CHASING
HUMILITY

"In *Chasing Humility*, Joel Stepanek does a masterful job giving the reader practical steps for cultivating authentic humility. Drawing on scripture, engaging stories, and good old common sense, this book is funny and wise, raw and relatable. Stepanek's insights offer a soul-stirring read to any soul looking to improve. The question isn't whether we need to be humble, but who can be humble enough to do something about it. This book is the perfect way to grow in holiness and ultimately, happiness, one achievable step at a time."

Mark Hart
Executive Vice President, Life Teen International

"This book was like a punch to the gut—a much needed, very welcome, life-changing gut punch. It is bold, honest, and raw. Joel has given us an absolutely delightful read that is also really challenging, and it is just what we (and so many others) need to be reminded of the necessity to live and walk humbly with the Lord. Read this book. Absorb this book. Let Joel and his words on humility sucker-punch you and you'll be so grateful."

Katie Prejean McGrady and Tommy McGrady
Catholic speakers and cohosts of *The Electric Waffle*

"Joel Stepanek highlights for us the proper and sacred space of humility in the Christian life. Exploring the Litany of Humility, he provides a delightful roadmap for embracing the virtue not as a weakness but as a strength in our personal prayer lives and leadership outreach. There could not be a better time for leaders to be reintroduced to the virtue of humility in a world that very often values self-centeredness over seeing and supporting others."

Rev. Dan Felton
Vicar General, Diocese of Green Bay

"Joel Stepanek's voice and vision are incredibly needed in the Catholic Church today. With clarity, joy, and a sharp intellect, he unpacks the virtue of humility in a way that is accessible and inspiring for people at all levels of faith. What a gift this book will be to anyone who picks it up!"

Emily Wilson Hussem
Catholic musician, speaker, and author of *Go Bravely*

CHASING HUMILITY

8 Ways to Shape a Christian Heart

Joel Stepanek

Ave Maria Press AVE Notre Dame, Indiana

Founded in 1865, Ave Maria Press is a ministry of the United States Province of Holy Cross.

www.avemariapress.com

Paperback: ISBN-13 978-1-59471-895-3

E-book: ISBN-13 978-1-59471-896-0

Cover design by Kristen Hornyak Bonelli.

Text design by Brianna Dombo.

Printed and bound in the United States of America.

Library of Congress Cataloging-in-Publication Data is available.

For Colleen,
whose humility and love continually inspire me
and reveal who Jesus is to me every day.

And to Leah and Ryan,
thank you for the push I needed to write this book.
Without your enthusiasm and encouragement,
it would not exist.

The secret of life lies in laughter and humility.
—G. K. Chesterton

CONTENTS

INTRODUCTION

I'm afraid of humility. I think most people are. I know this because when I told people I was writing a book, they were excited. When I told them the book was about humility, their faces dropped and many tried to find a way to talk about something else. Some said, "Oh," and then pulled out their phone like an important text was coming in. They had no interest in a book about humility. Humility is not attractive. Humility is hard.

We are repelled by or afraid of humility because we don't get it. The prospect of being humble conjures up images of letting other people walk all over us, never accepting praise, and rejecting wealth, affirmation, maybe even love. Humble people don't need those things. Who would want to be humble if it means living your life in the dirt? But I've learned that if I want to be successful in anything, humility is key.

It's taken me nearly twenty years to be able to write that line and really believe it, but that doesn't make me any less afraid of humility.

I'm not sure how the idea that being humble was to be a failure developed in my mind. Probably a lot of things contributed. Both my parents were faithful Christians; we prayed every night as a family, and they made sure that they taught us about the faith and spoke about Jesus. But my family was not successful in the worldly sense. We didn't have a lot of money. My parents worked hard—but success wasn't something we had when it came to money, status, or fame.

I remember my mom once telling me that when we really love the Lord, we are humbled and sometimes we suffer. I know that statement stuck with me.

When I was sixteen years old I attended a youth conference, and during the keynote address the speaker called out from the stage: "The key to our faith is humility! Without a humble heart, we can't really follow Jesus." The words of my mother echoed in my head and I started to put the pieces together—humility meant suffering, and that was the way we became real disciples of Jesus.

In college I worked at a tanning salon and a gym—not places considered synonymous with humility. There were a lot of good people at those places, but also a lot of vain, prideful people. Being that close to the ugliness of pride pushed me toward a greater rejection of it. I used to daydream about preaching humility to every orange-colored body builder I met so that they would repent of their prideful ways and embrace humility by eating a bacon double cheeseburger with extra mayo (mayonnaise being, in my opinion, the worst of all condiments).

In my last semester of college, I wrote a paper for my New Testament studies course about Jesus' teachings on humility. I talked about how wealth (and, in my mind, success) prevents people from getting into heaven. So, those who want to follow Jesus need to let everything go. I concluded that those who seek worldly success are forfeiting their passage into heaven.

I was missing the mark at every turn. In hindsight, I realize that I had developed my own definition of humility, especially in my walk of faith. Nobody had defined humility for me, let alone told me what it meant to live a humble life. I came to believe that you were either successful in the eyes of the world or you were humble and destitute but you got to be a disciple of Jesus. You were either full of yourself and prideful, or despised yourself and were humble. I couldn't see a way to balance those things; humility meant losing everything you had, including your desires, hopes, dreams, and plans, and letting God do whatever he wanted with you. I assumed that whatever God wanted for you was probably going to be terrible. I reasoned that if God really loved you (and you really loved God), he showed that to you by making you live a super-crummy life, and because you loved God you were content with your super-crummy life. I once heard a priest refer to this mindset as "the Gospel of Suck."

By the time I left college, I considered myself a bold missionary ready to serve and make no money; I was ready to be a beautiful failure in the eyes of the world, but confident in the glorious triumph of heaven. I was ready to live the Gospel of Suck and proclaim it to all, hoping they would join me.

But then I started to succeed in the things I did. I wasn't seeking affirmation or fame; I was just working hard. Forgive me, Lord, for I wasn't trying to succeed—I was trying to fail and be humble to show how much I loved you.

WORTH DOING WELL

My dad used to tell me, "Any job worth doing is worth doing well." His favorite time to drop this dad phrase was after I did a terrible job mowing the lawn. This was his way of saying, "Guess what you get to spend your afternoon doing? You get to redo the lawn because you did it poorly the first time."

I hated that saying, but it stuck with me. No matter how hard I tried not to seek success in order to remain humble, something inside me wanted the work I did to matter, and I wanted to do it well.

When you work hard, I found out, you may *actually* succeed. And make money.

And be recognized and affirmed and reach many other markers of success that I thought a good Christian avoided. And that scared me. I was failing at living out the Gospel of Suck.

So, I became incredibly scrupulous. I didn't want to become prideful because I knew that was the path toward total ruin. I stopped taking compliments. Conversations in which someone tried to compliment me became incredibly awkward, even painful, running something like this: "Oh, don't thank me. I'm a depraved human, capable of no good. This is 100 percent God.

Any involvement I had was accidental. In fact, there must be some mistake because the nice things you are saying feel like needles against my humble skin."

People eventually got discouraged when they tried to affirm or thank me for the work I was doing. I wasn't enjoyable to serve with because I always looked for and exaggerated what went wrong—like a humble guy should do, right? I often began conversations by saying negative things about myself. I thought that was humility—making myself lower than someone else—and so I made sure to beat myself down whenever I could.

All of that was pretty exhausting, but I continued to work hard, bringing more success. Inside me there was an incredible tension. On the one hand, I wanted to live up to the ideals of humility that I had developed in my mind. On the other hand, I was realizing that hard work brings success, that some career choices can provide a decent living, and that sometimes people who love us actually want to praise and affirm who we are. It was dawning on me that all of these things can happen while we follow Jesus.

I don't think I'm alone in this tension. I have observed that when it comes to humility, most of us fall into one of two camps. Many dedicated Christians, including me, find themselves stuck in the Gospel of Suck camp. We know that we should take the yoke of Jesus, who is meek and humble of heart, upon us—but we also feel called to be doctors or other professionals, and they make a lot more money than missionaries. How do people in this camp reconcile this tension? We wonder if we ought to follow our career path—become lawyers, work in finance, run businesses—but then volunteer all of our spare time in a developing nation. People in the Gospel of Suck camp struggle with how to handle genuine compliments. Should we blow them off? Should we respond by telling people how terrible we actually are? Often our response to affirmation is to become negative and standoffish, and to look for reasons to focus on the bad things of life. If we make money, we can't enjoy it. If we get compliments, we reject them. We tend to be sharply judgmental of people that are joyful because, really, how can you be joyful *and* humble?

The second camp pushes that tension aside completely. They are the Humility Sucks camp. They've written humility off as archaic and weird, something they don't really get so they do their own thing. They aren't professional-sports-player prideful, but they know the hustle and are pretty proud of what they've done. They look fondly on their accomplishments and make sure other people know about them. They don't want coworkers and management to forget how awesome they are because when people remember your job performance it means job stability. They reason that humility might be good for those that serve the Church—priests, nuns, monks—but not for the rest of us.

The problem with both camps is that they are prideful and neglect God. The attitude of the first camp—the Gospel of Suck—is really just false pride and can have disastrous effects on our relationship with God. Think about it this way—a child comes up to you with a picture she made. She is so proud of her creation and wants to show it to you. Instead of praising it, though, you point out all the flaws. You tell her that there are other pictures way better than this one—even other pictures she has drawn that she should try to imitate. You suggest she take an art class or, better yet, find another hobby she can succeed at. That's a recipe for a crying child. No decent human does that to an excited kid.

That's how we treat ourselves sometimes. God created us as unique, once-in-a-universe occurrences and loves us just as we are. But some of us look at God's creation in the mirror and only find flaws, somehow believing God wants us to do that. And then we make the mistake of feeling content or even smug in our supposed humility. We aren't being humble—we are, in fact, being prideful and self-absorbed.

Christian author G. K. Chesterton responded to this mentality with a famous line defining humility: "Humility is not thinking less of yourself, but thinking of yourself less."

The Humility Sucks camp misses out on the freedom that true humility brings. In rejecting humility, we embrace pride as we turn inward. We see ourselves as the masters of our own destiny, worried that living humility will result in our downfall. When we shun humility in favor of pride, we slowly imprison ourselves. Pride is lonely; when we rely only on our gifts, talents, and abilities, we miss the community that is created when we ask for help. When we refuse to be humble, we become fearful of the ways that others may surpass us one day. We live in anxiety, tension, and isolation.

AT THE ROOT OF TENSION

Pride is considered a capital sin because it rejects God and other people in favor of self-reliance. When we are prideful, we get to make the rules. We rely on ourselves as our own masters and rulers. We don't accept help or community from other people, unless it puts us further ahead. Pride leads to other sins as we reject God's commands and see other people as a means to our own selfish ends. We look at our gifts and talents, our accomplishments and successes, and say, "I did that. There might not be an 'I' in team, but there is a 'me,' and that was all me." Sinful pride causes us to believe that we are our own saviors.

We can keep up our prideful attitude for a while. We can hustle on our own gifts and talents, promoting ourselves to other people and working our way up the ladder. We may even seem successful to others, but eventually life crumbles. It may not be in a horrific, celebrity financial collapse sort of way, but at the end of our lives death comes and we realize something: We can't save ourselves. All our success, wealth, and recognition mean nothing in our final moments. St. Vincent de Paul wrote, "Humility is nothing but truth, and pride is nothing but lying." If we believe we can save ourselves, at the end of our lives we will reap the fruit of that lie. We are not our own saviors, and we cannot escape death.

We need the Savior—we can't do this all on our own. Our gifts and talents (which lead to our successes and accomplishments) are given by God and cultivated with his help.

How do we balance humility between the extremes of pride and self-deprecation? How do we accept the realities of success, money, even fame and power, and still live as Christian disciples? Is that even possible? Attaining humility can seem like a hopeless chase; we aren't sure what to look for, but we know we should pursue it.

The correct understanding of humility is the key to, well, everything. If we want to be successful in any arena of life—a job, marriage, our friendships, and most especially our prayer and relationship with God—we need to understand and live humility. Being authentically humble doesn't require that we avoid success—it actually drives us *to be successful.*

Think for a moment about great world leaders—the ones that really made a difference and an impact on history. There are many whose names we know and many more we will never know but whose impact is felt. Those people—such as Dr. Martin Luther King Jr., Mahatma Gandhi, and St. Teresa of Calcutta—understood and lived humility.

"OK," you may be thinking, "those are all religious activist leaders. Two embraced poverty, and all lived through a time of incredible social instability and upheaval." But strip away the externals—focus on their leadership. What made them great leaders? Could it have been their humility?

In a recent study using data from six countries, the leadership group Catalyst demonstrated that humility is one of the key traits in good business leadership. Jim Collins, author of the wildly successful business book *Good to Great,* said that Level 5 leaders (the most successful) are the only leaders capable of taking a company from good to great. He says that the key trait differentiating them from Level 4 leaders is humility. You can't achieve lasting success without humility.

Humility is key in marriage. If one spouse dominates the relationship and refuses to admit being wrong, always imposing their own will and never learning or growing, then that marriage isn't going to last. Infidelity is often listed as the number-one reason for divorce, and at its core, infidelity is about pride. It is one partner saying, "My feelings/wants/desires matter more than yours." The most satisfying relationships of any type are marked by humility.

In our walk with Jesus, humility is essential. Humility is the foundation of prayer and discipleship. It is the acknowledgment that we are not God and the acceptance of who we are before God. True humility is embracing the fact that God is the Creator and we are the created. God sustains us and loves us. Humility puts us in right relationship with God. Without it, we can't follow or accept God's will.

Humility, when practiced well, doesn't lower our self-esteem; it actually produces confidence. In fact, there is no other way to be truly confident in yourself than to be humble.

AN OLD PRAYER FOR MODERN TIMES

A few years after my college graduation, I found a road map for learning true humility. A friend recommended that I pray the "Litany of Humility." This is a short prayer consisting of petitions to Jesus. Through it, we first ask Jesus to remove desires from our hearts. Then we ask Jesus to deliver us from fears. Finally, we petition Jesus to give us new desires. Here is the full text of the prayer:

O Jesus! meek and humble of heart,
Hear me.

From the desire of being esteemed,
Deliver me, Jesus. *(Repeat for the following petitions.)*
From the desire of being loved . . .
From the desire of being extolled . . .
From the desire of being honored . . .
From the desire of being praised . . .
From the desire of being preferred to others . . .
From the desire of being consulted . . .
From the desire of being approved . . .

From the fear of being humiliated . . .
Deliver me, Jesus. *(Repeat for the following petitions.)*
From the fear of being despised . . .
From the fear of suffering rebukes . . .
From the fear of being calumniated . . .
From the fear of being forgotten . . .
From the fear of being ridiculed . . .
From the fear of being wronged . . .
From the fear of being suspected . . .

That others may be loved more than I,
Jesus, grant me the grace to desire it. *(Repeat for the*
following petitions.)
That others may be esteemed more than I . . .
That, in the opinion of the world, others may increase
and I may decrease . . .
That others may be chosen and I set aside . . .
That others may be praised and I unnoticed . . .
That others may be preferred to me in everything . . .
That others may become holier than I, provided that
I may become as holy as I should . . .

At first, I prayed this litany every morning and tried to
be mindful throughout the day of ways that I acted humbly.
I noticed subtle changes—grace always changes us—but as I
prayed over time, I noticed a pattern within the prayer. This

pattern provided me with a reflective and practical framework to become genuinely humble.

DESIRING THE WRONG THINGS

In the first part of the Litany of Humility, we ask Jesus to deliver us from particular desires with the formula *"From the desire of* (insert prideful thing here), *deliver me, Jesus."* Desire isn't a bad thing in itself, but if our desire becomes disordered, or if we are directing our desire at the wrong thing, then we need to be freed of it.

Think about our desire to be loved. We all want to be loved, but when we are willing to do anything to be loved, or we focus more on how much people love us than on how we love others, then that good desire works against us. It hurts our relationships and keeps us from serving, leading, and working effectively. It hinders us from knowing Jesus because our attention and first concerns are directed toward ourselves.

So we pray against that disordered desire, trusting that Jesus hears our prayer and will answer it. But as soon as one demon goes, another one steps in to take its place. That demon is fear.

BE NOT AFRAID

In the second part of the Litany of Humility, we ask for deliverance from specific fears with the formula *"From the fear of* (insert feared thing here), *deliver me, Jesus."*

When we have disordered desires for a long time, they can be hard to let go of, and doing so leaves an empty space in that part of our lives. We don't like empty spaces. They make us afraid. That's why the second set of petitions we pray involve fear. Think about what happens when we let go of our desire to be loved; what do we fear? We fear that we will be alone or even hated. People may do the opposite of love us, and that is scary, especially if we have spent a lot of time trying to win the love of others.

People who have gone through a 12-step program know the reality of empty space. They've formed routines around harmful addictions, and they know that if they get clean but don't change the routines—the way they walk home, the people they hang out with, what they look at online—they will fall back into addiction. They need to fill the empty space in their lives with something new—a new routine—in order to stay sober.

CREATE A NEW HEART IN ME

In the third part of the Litany of Humility, we pray for a change of heart with the words *"Jesus, grant me the grace to desire it."* We ask God to reorder our desires so that they become good again and not destructive. King David asks God for a change of heart in Psalm 51: "A clean heart create for me, God; renew within me a steadfast spirit" (v. 12).

These desires are something new that counteract the disordered desires from which we ask to be delivered. After we pray *against* the desire to be loved and the fear of being despised, for example, we pray *for* the desire that others may be loved more than us. Here is where it gets practical: We are responsible to act on the grace we receive through these petitions. We can choose to love others as ourselves. We can go out of our way to love those around us. We can make others feel loved. And those desires replace the desires that are out of whack and confront our fear of being alone or despised.

We can rearrange all the petitions in the Litany of Humility in this way. We can ask for a desire to be taken away, for protection against a fear that can sneak into the void, and then for Jesus to fill us with a new desire. I've grouped petitions from the first, second, and third sections of the litany and tied them to a particular practice we can engage in to be more humble. These practices form a solid foundation for humility and for real success—the kind that changes our leadership, relationships, and spirituality from good to great. This is how I've rearranged the petitions with a corresponding trait of humility.

Being Authentic:
From the desire of being esteemed,
  Deliver me, Jesus.
From the fear of being wronged,
  Deliver me, Jesus.
That I may become as holy as I should,
  Jesus, grant me the grace to desire it.

Growing Confidence:
From the desire of being preferred to others,
  Deliver me, Jesus.
From the fear of being humiliated,
  Deliver me, Jesus.
That others may be esteemed more than I,
  Jesus, grant me the grace to desire it.

Being Grateful for Today:
From the desire of being honored,
  Deliver me, Jesus.
From the fear of being calumniated,
  Deliver me, Jesus.
That, in the opinion of the world, others may increase
  and I may decrease,
  Jesus, grant me the grace to desire it.

Loving Others:
From the desire of being loved,
  Deliver me, Jesus.
From the fear of being despised,
  Deliver me, Jesus.
That others may be loved more than I,
  Jesus, grant me the grace to desire it.

Giving Praise:
From the desire of being praised,
> Deliver me, Jesus.

From the fear of suffering rebukes,
> Deliver me, Jesus.

That others may be praised and I unnoticed,
> Jesus, grant me the grace to desire it.

Empowering Those around Me:
From the desire of being extolled,
> Deliver me, Jesus.

From the fear of being forgotten,
> Deliver me, Jesus.

That others may be preferred to me in everything,
> Jesus, grant me the grace to desire it.

Becoming the Mentor:
From the desire of being consulted,
> Deliver me, Jesus.

From the fear of being suspected,
> Deliver me, Jesus.

That others may be chosen and I set aside,
> Jesus, grant me the grace to desire it.

Breaking Boundaries:
From the desire of being approved,
> Deliver me, Jesus.

From the fear of being ridiculed,
> Deliver me, Jesus.

That others may become holier than I,
> Jesus, grant me the grace to desire it.

Some of the following chapters are easy to read, but others will be a struggle because they strike at the heart of pride. If we believe what Jesus tells us, that "whatever you ask in my name, I will do" (Jn 14:13; see also Matthew 7:7), then we should approach this prayer for humility with reverence (and, honestly, excitement), because Jesus can change our lives through it. If we are sincere about the prayer, there will be parts that make us pause for a moment and ask, "Wait, do I really want this?"

That's a good question, and it tests our trust in Jesus that he knows what is best for our holiness. That is why we begin our prayer with a petition directly to Christ.

THE CHASE IS ON

If we are going to chase humility, we need to be open to redefining it and becoming aware of aspects of Jesus that are new to us. We need to identify where we struggle and where we can grow. It is a journey that we embark on; don't expect perfection immediately. As we break open sets of petitions from the Litany of Humility, focusing on key traits of humility that we are trying to emulate, we must peel back the layers of pride that exist in our lives. That takes honesty.

At the beginning of each chapter I present the set of petitions keyed to a particular aspect of humility. Pray through these lines and ask yourself, "Am I completely open to what Jesus may do through these petitions, or am I only seeing Jesus as I want to see him?" Can you say, "This chapter is for me. I am going to be totally affirmed in my life, right now"? Will you say, "Lord, I can grow in these areas"? Or will you say, "I trust you, Lord, but not if it means (insert your boundary here). You couldn't possibly mean that, though, right?" Or will you grow fearful and say, "I don't know if I can pray this with my whole heart. Do I really want what Jesus will give me and the new thing he will do in my life with this petition?"

Jesus only wills our good. He didn't come to destroy what is good in us; he came to liberate us from sin. He came to help us become holy and whole. Humility is simply the disposition to allow that great work to take place.

If you are ready to redefine humility and move beyond what you think you know, then it's time to get started. Chasing humility is about more than fulfilling a set of rules; it is about finding out who we really are. Let's get running.

Weekly Humility Practice

Spend fifteen to twenty minutes each day reading from the Bible. Start with the gospels. When we read about the life of Christ, we begin to correct the errant images we have of Jesus and learn about the God we worship.

Monthly Humility Practice

Commit thirty minutes to silent prayer. Don't journal, engage in active prayer, or bring anything to read. Simply sit and contemplate the reality that God is God, and you are not.

Yearly Humility Practice

Make an annual retreat—even if it is only a day long—to get away from your daily routines and reconnect with Jesus. Meditate on the question that Jesus asked Peter, "Who do you say that I am?"

1.
BEING AUTHENTIC

From the desire of being esteemed,
Deliver me, Jesus.
From the fear of being wronged,
Deliver me, Jesus.
That I may become as holy as I should,
Jesus, grant me the grace to desire it.

Three hours. That's how long I engaged in a conversation with a friend before he asked me anything about my life. We went a full three hours as he told me about work, taxes, his pets, and an online course he was taking. It was only as an afterthought that he asked, "So, what's new with you?"

But it was hopeless. After a few sentences my friend grew visibly anxious and used something I said as a springboard into some more details about his life. By the end of the night I was exhausted and practically pushed him out the door.

We all know people like this—the kind of people that we dread speaking with because we know the conversation is going to revolve around them and we are going to be left nodding our head without saying much of anything.

It is easy to get frustrated by these people. After all, we want to be known and to celebrate our accomplishments, share those things that make us happy, and talk about ourselves. In the midst of a friend's monologue of self-praise, we find ourselves asking, "What about me? Don't you care about my life?"

Interestingly, our frustration is perhaps as self-centered as the people that frustrate us. Shouldn't they at least ask about us? Our lives are amazing! We want to talk about our experiences.

Why do we do this? Why do we want to talk more about ourselves than about other people? Why do we wait for our turn to speak rather than really listening to the people we are having a conversation with? It comes down to something very simple— we want others to admire us. We want them to respect who we are. We want them to leave a conversation thinking better of us than they did before.

NOT-SO-SECRET ADMIRER

There are lots of reasons that we think this way. In a work environment, we want other people to know what we do so that we will appear needed and our jobs will be secure. Our conversations therefore revolve around justifying our jobs. When I graduated from college, I began work in a parish and was surprised at how much our staff meetings were simply to-do lists from every person. We all talked about how busy we were and how important our work was. I don't think this is isolated to a church environment. When people feel insecure about their jobs, they utilize any opportunity to justify what they do. It isn't just the annoying people at work—you and I do it, too. We just might not do it at staff meetings.

There are a few ways we work to get the admiration of others. We want people to admire how busy we are, so we talk about how much we have to do. We want people to admire how we strive on in difficult circumstances, so we talk about how hard our lives are. We want people to compliment our accomplishments, so we make sure that we share them often. We want to be liked—so we present a version of ourselves that we think people will like. We amplify our quality features and downplay the tough ones.

People have been crafting their personality to please others forever, but modern technology allows us to (literally) place filters on our lives to help us manage what other people see. As social media use has risen, our ability to connect has dropped. If you are over the age of twenty-five, don't write this off as a teenage problem; older adults struggle with appropriate social media use just as much as teenagers. Thanks to social media, talking about ourselves has risen to a whole new level. Our entire platform is about us. Now social media has even moved away from the term *friends* for people we connect with, preferring *followers*. How disconnected and self-affirming is that language? People judge their worth on how many likes a post gets, evaluating everything from their appearance to their job based on the opinions of other people.

FROM THE DESIRE OF BEING ESTEEMED

The desire to be liked is a basic human desire; being liked means that we stay with the in crowd versus being isolated. In the Litany of Humility, the expression we use for being liked is "being esteemed." Our desire for admiration and affirmation really boils down to a desire to win the esteem of other people. The petition we pray regarding that desire is, *"From the desire of being esteemed, deliver me, Jesus."*

There is something very devastating about changing who we are, crafting a false personality, or hiding parts of ourselves so that people will think better of us. It is deceitful to the people we are in relationships with, and it also has a profound impact on our own mental health and our relationship with God. When we so deeply desire affirmation that we present a false self to the world, we risk losing ourselves and we experience cognitive dissonance. We act as though we are more put together than we know we are.

PERSONALITY DISSONANCE

During my sophomore year of high school, I went through a chaotic period (who didn't?). It was a normal teenage experience; I was trying to find out who I was and determine my place in the world. The psychologist Erik Erikson called identity formation the key developmental task of adolescence. As teenagers, we spend most of our time trying to answer the question, "Who am I?" This questioning continues through our twenties, but by our thirties our identities are fairly well formed. We move on to other developmental tasks, such as intimacy and generativity.

This doesn't mean the question "Who am I?" goes away completely, though. We may still ask it, especially when our life changes—a job loss, a divorce, a disruption in a friendship, a shift in our health. When we answer this question from a firm foundation, our lives are more peaceful. But if we are crafting our identity based on what other people like or esteem, we are setting ourselves up for a fall. As a teenager, I found myself in that place. I crafted unique personas for different groups of people, all in the name of being liked. The result was a breakdown in epic teenage fashion. During that period I had a conversation with my dad, and the advice he gave I've not forgotten.

He said, "There are three parts to who we are. There is what we see and say about ourselves. There is how we want others to see us—the kind of person that we present to the world. And then there is who God says that I am. That is the most important part, because what God tells us is true. If those three areas don't line up, our life is in dissonance, and we won't know who we are and we won't be happy."

What my dad was talking about was authenticity. He was talking about being who we really are—and at that time in my life (and many times after that) I was just trying to be liked. When I find myself striving for the esteem of others rather than holding firm to my foundations, I return to those three questions to bring myself back to authenticity:

- Who does God say that I am?
- What do I say about myself?
- How do I want other people to see me?

When I ask those three questions, I quickly find areas of misalignment in my life. They stand out like red flags, and they all lead back to my desire to be esteemed and respected by others.

Who Does God Say That I Am? This is a set truth. God speaks promises to us, revealed in the pages of sacred scripture, and his Word is true. God says that you are known (see Psalm 139:1) and you are loved (see 1 John 4:19). God calls us his beloved sons and daughters (see Galatians 3:26 and 2 Corinthians 6:18). Nothing exists that can make God love you less or separate his love from you (see Romans 8:38–39). When God looks at you, he says that you are loved, accepted, and valued no matter what. God wants what is best for us, and calls us out of sin to live in freedom. We have to begin with this truth.

What Do I Say about Myself? If we are loved and valued by God, then what we say about ourselves should be positive, although we may struggle with flaws and imperfections. What we say about ourselves relates to how we've answered the question, "Who am I?" If we have a positive self-image, we are less likely to compromise our identity for the sake of being esteemed. If we have a low self-image, we may try to hide or change who we are in order to get people to affirm us.

How Do I Want Other People to See Me? This question should not be confused with the question, "How do other people see me?" though we can certainly use the perception of others as a way of testing how authentic we are. If one of our core values is to be always joyful, but the perception of other people is that we are pessimistic, melancholic, and frustrated, then we are failing at authenticity. However, this type of test isn't foolproof. We can't control what people think about us, and some people might have the wrong idea about who we are, despite our best efforts. Asking ourselves how we want others to see us has to do with the persona we cultivate in real and digital life—often done in the name of getting people to like and appreciate us.

These three questions form a Venn diagram of authenticity. When all the areas come together, we are living in harmony. Unfortunately, our desire to be esteemed can easily throw these areas out of alignment and result in personality dissonance.

VANITY AND EMPTINESS

When our answers to the questions "What do I say about myself?" and "How do I want other people to see me?" line up, but they don't line up with who God says we are, then we experience vanity. Vanity is often associated with beauty, but the word comes from the Latin root *vanus*, which means "empty." The writer of the book of Ecclesiastes remarked, "Vanity of vanities! All things are vanity!" (1:2). Without God's truth in our lives, we are ultimately empty. Even if what we say about ourselves is consistent with what we present to others, when it is out of alignment with who God says we are, we find ourselves empty. Many people have pursued a path in life that from the outside looked consistent, but in the end found themselves empty. Our desire to be liked can cause us to forget God's truth and change our perception of our identity in order that others will hold us in high esteem.

BROKEN AND ISOLATED

When our answers to the questions "Who does God say that I am?" and "How do I want other people to see me?" line up, but they don't align with what we say about ourselves, we feel lost and broken. This often occurs when we experience a disorder such as anxiety or depression. We may know the truth that God speaks about us, and we may project that to others, but under the surface we are hurting. We don't feel like ourselves. Knowing the truth and projecting the truth are one thing, but what we believe about the truth is a different story. I've struggled in my life with depression and anxiety, and there are many times when I knew in my head what God thought about me. I projected that to other people and tried to live it publicly. But when I looked at myself in the mirror, I said very different things. The result was isolation. I needed to admit that I was hurting, but I didn't want other people to see that, so I wound up being isolated. I started to believe the lies I told myself and simply felt alone.

I worried that admitting the truth of my illness to others would cause them to lose respect for me. I worried that if I told people I struggled with how I viewed myself, they would judge me or think less of me. My desire to be esteemed kept me trapped in depression for many years until I received encouragement from good friends to find help.

A DOUBLE LIFE

Sometimes our answers to the questions, "What do I say about myself?" and "Who does God say that I am?" line up, but don't align with how we want other people to see us. We know the truth, but are afraid of letting other people see it because we are worried they might not like it. So we start to live a double life. At the most innocent, a double life consists of simply not talking about our faith and compartmentalizing important parts of who we are. This is bigger than emphasizing different traits around different people—we all do that. My coworkers know me in a slightly different capacity than some of my friends outside of work. My wife knows me in a way that some of my friends don't. That simply represents healthy boundaries in relationships.

We get into trouble when we suppress or even change who we fundamentally are in the presence of other people. If our faith is important to us, but when we are out with people we stop praying before meals, lie about our involvement with a church, or even enter into harsh conversations about faith, then we are living a double life. At the worst, we act differently around other people, betraying our core values in the interest of being liked. An easy way to root out this behavior is to ask your friends, coworkers, or even family members to identify your core values. If the person they describe to you doesn't match those values, then you may be living a double life.

Our misaligned behavior in these three areas stems from a desire to be esteemed, admired, and respected. In vanity, we think highly of ourselves and pride runs deep. We believe we are masters of our own fortune, self-made individuals that control our own lives. We talk about ourselves often as we seek the admiration of others.

When we are lost and broken, we hesitate to let anyone in because we don't want them to see us as vulnerable and messy. We worry that if we let them in, they will lose respect for us, think we are weak, or may even try to hurt us—using our weakness to their advantage. I spoke to a friend about the climate at the company she worked for. She said no person wanted to be vulnerable and speak about challenges they faced because management would question their fitness for the job. As a result, coworkers never discussed challenges or obstacles. Everyone presented a rose-colored version of work, but beneath the surface they were all struggling.

In our double lives, we put filters on—sometimes literally. Have you ever heard the word "catfishing"? In catfishing, an individual creates an entirely different persona online and interacts with others under that persona—even engaging in romantic online relationships. Most of us don't go to that extreme, but just because our profile bears our real name doesn't mean it accurately represents us. It represents a curated collection of our best moments, happiest news, or distressing incidents meant to prompt people to admire us.

We desire to be esteemed, but that desire can get out of control and lead to vanity, brokenness, and living a double life. Our desire comes from something deeper—we are afraid of being hurt.

FROM THE FEAR
OF BEING WRONGED

In the Litany of Humility, we pray against the desire to be esteemed, but we also pray against the fear of being wronged. We do this with the petition, *"From the fear of being wronged, deliver me, Jesus."*

Living our lives authentically involves vulnerability. When we allow people to see us as we are without adding filters or curating our lives, we take a risk. Suddenly there are no walls to hide behind. We are exposed, and we start to fear, "What if I don't measure up? What if someone tries to hurt me with what they know about me? What if people stop respecting me because of my beliefs or my past?" When we drop our desire to be esteemed in favor of authenticity, we risk being wronged.

You may have painful memories of letting someone in and being vulnerable with them, only to be hurt by that person. Maybe you just tried to be yourself but were shut down by a group of friends. When I finally got the courage to tell my college girlfriend how important my faith was to me—something I had hidden from her—she dumped me about a week later. She said that it was weird. That hurt. It made me afraid to let people into such an intimate part of my life after that.

Vulnerability and authenticity go hand in hand, but they aren't forms of weakness. They actually provide strength and clarity. They help us to know who we are, where we stand with others, and where others stand with us. In a work setting, authentic leaders that aren't afraid to be vulnerable are the most well respected. In relationships, authenticity and vulnerability lead to deeper intimacy. Authenticity is a foundational trait for the humble Christian and has a profound impact on how we work, engage in relationships, and live our faith. It begins with our relationship with God; if we want to become holy, we need to live authentically.

THAT I MAY BECOME
AS HOLY AS I SHOULD

You were created by God—and God loves you. God sees you for who you are, and God wants you to base what you think about yourself and how you present yourself to others on that truth.

Living that truth is called holiness. A lot of things may come to mind when we say the word "holy." We may think of religious icons, of saints, or of someone we know who spends a lot of time at church or in the service of others. But being holy is simply living out who God made you to be. It is loving others and loving yourself. It is knowing Jesus Christ and following him.

We pray that we might become holy with the last petition of the Litany of Humility, "*That others may become holier than I, provided that I may become as holy as I should.*" The entirety of the litany leads up to this petition, so we are going to break it into two parts, one at the beginning of our journey and one at the end. For authenticity, we focus on the latter half of the petition, "*that I may become as holy as I should.*"

I've found that a lot of people have a distorted view of what it means to be holy—myself included. We think that when we start following Jesus, we need to change and become someone different. We think that we need to act another way or be a different person in order to impress Jesus. Jesus becomes one more person that we want to admire and respect us. When we think that way, we start to focus on what we might do for Jesus so that he will like us. We imagine Jesus sitting in heaven and looking at us and saying, "Wow, look at what she is doing! That's amazing—I love and respect her way more, now."

Nothing you do can make Jesus love you more or less. Many adults don't grasp this reality. You can't earn God's love, and you can't lose it. It is constant. God sees every aspect of your life—even the hairs on your head are counted (see Luke 12:7). God always has access to the innermost parts of our hearts.

A popular expression in Christian circles is to "let Jesus into our hearts," as though Jesus did not already have the ability to see into who we are. It isn't a matter of letting Jesus into our hearts so much as opening up to what he wants to do. Allowing God to do work within us is a risky exercise. We may find out that there are some things we need to change. We may have to drop some bad behaviors and be more authentic with others. We may need to attend therapy so we can have a better view of ourselves. We may realize that we need to pray more and spend more time with Christ in quiet contemplation.

But if we focus on what we are going to do for God, rather than what God wants to do for us, we become inauthentic. We become blind to God's love, regardless of the mess we are in.

I SAW THAT

When I first began public speaking on a regular basis, I attended a luncheon at an event with several people that I really admired and respected. I was in the worst location for an introvert—at the middle of the long restaurant table. I find that spot nerve-racking because conversations are going on in front of you and to the sides. Instead of engaging with only one or two people, you potentially have five people to talk with. That number goes up if others on the outer reaches crane their necks to lean into an ongoing conversation. On top of that, if you aren't talking to anyone, it looks really obvious. That is a lot to navigate!

Fate put me at the middle of the table, and I sat in awe of the people around me as I did my best to make conversation. Our waiter hadn't come to offer drinks yet, but the anxiety of being at the middle of the table and the multiple conversations I was involved in left my throat dry. I picked up my glass of water without realizing how much condensation was on the sides and it slipped out of my hand, spilling water all over the table.

I was mortified. Then I realized that everyone around me was engrossed in conversation. It was an introvert's dream—I made a huge blunder and nobody noticed! But now I faced a dilemma: The area in front of me was covered with water, ice, and a single wedge of lemon, and it wouldn't be long before a lull in the conversation turned the attention back to me and the giant mess on the table. I acted fast and reached my arms out like I was about to hug my grandmother, put my forearms down on the table to act as shovels, and scooped all of the water, ice, and that one lemon wedge directly into my lap and out of sight.

It was ice cold, but I didn't care. I hoped that by the time the meal was over my pants would be dry and nobody would know that I dropped that water glass. It didn't escape the view of one person, though.

Steve, one of the executives at the company where I worked, was sitting right across from me, and when I made eye contact with him, he was smiling and chuckling to himself. But it wasn't a mean smile or laugh. It was like he was saying, "I totally get where you are right now, how you feel, and how awful what just happened was. But it is also really funny, and I've been there." Something about it was reassuring. He handed me a napkin and said, still smiling, "I saw that."

It didn't diminish what he thought of me. He didn't make fun of me. He never brought it up to anyone else at the table, nor did he call attention to it. He offered me something to help clean up.

Steve helped me understand something about God in that moment. God sees you. He really sees you. He knows all the good things and all the bad things. He knows the mess you put yourself in. He knows the ways you try to hide it from others. It doesn't make him love you less; it makes him want to help clean you up.

When Steve offered me the napkin, I could have played dumb and rejected it despite the evidence around me and the uncomfortable expression on my face. If I had done that, Steve probably would have honored it and let me sit in my mess. He wasn't going to push or be forceful or demand that I stand up so that I could dry off.

A MODEL OF AUTHENTIC VULNERABILITY

Jesus sees our circumstances, but it is up to us to be authentic and vulnerable about them. In the Gospel of Mark, chapter five, Jesus heals two people in a row. He is on his way to heal a synagogue official's daughter, but on the way something unexpected happens. A woman who has been ill for twelve years approaches Jesus. She has heard about his incredible power to heal the sick. She reasons that if she can get close enough to touch him, this might be enough to bring the healing to her body that many doctors failed to provide.

The woman faces challenges. There is a crowd around Jesus and, no doubt, the disciples are doing their best to clear a path and protect their teacher. In spite of this, the woman presses in and manages to touch Jesus' cloak. Miraculously, she is healed.

Jesus knows what is happening, though. He turns to the disciples to ask who touched him, and the disciples scoff. With so many people around, how can Jesus possibly think they can say who touched him? But the woman hears and confesses. At this point in the story, Mark inserts a unique line: "The woman, realizing what had happened to her, approached in fear and trembling. She fell down before Jesus and told him the whole truth" (Mk 5:33).

That statement, "she . . . told him the whole truth," is fascinating. Mark makes a point to say that she told him everything there was to know and held nothing back. She was authentic before Jesus, and her faith healed her.

We may seek healing from Jesus in prayer, or desire that God will change our life circumstances, but how often are we authentic and real with the Lord about our mess? In our effort to get Jesus to like us, we don't bring those messy pieces to prayer. We hide them, afraid to reach out in faith. We don't want to give God the whole truth, but some version of the truth that keeps us from facing reality.

We don't need to seek the esteem of God—God loves us. He doesn't want to see us broken or in sin, but he respects our decision to stay in our mess. We need to have the courage of that woman to trust that Jesus can heal us, and as we approach him to be prepared with the whole truth of our messes.

When we begin with that level of humility with the Lord, we will surely experience an impact on our relationships and our work ethic.

VULNERABLE RELATIONSHIPS

Authenticity in our relationships requires vulnerability and leads to intimacy. The word "intimacy" is easy to get hung up on. We often think of it with an overtly sexual connotation, but intimacy is more than that. The root of "intimacy" is *intimus*—a Latin word that means "innermost." We experience intimacy with someone when we know their innermost being. So, while intimacy can relate to sexuality, it doesn't always (just as many kinds of sexual behavior are not actually intimate). We reach a state of intimacy with another person when we know who they really are—they allow us into their innermost self.

Of course, once someone is in that innermost part of our heart, they can do much more damage than if we kept them at a safe distance. It also means they see the parts of us that aren't as flashy or exciting. They may see our failures and know our hurts. We take a risk in letting people see that vulnerable side of ourselves. We risk them walking away, taking part of us with them.

We need to have appropriate boundaries with other people and within our relationships. We can't let everyone into our deepest secrets—in fact, that is an unhealthy approach to authenticity. Being authentic is simply being ourselves and not trying to create a false persona that other people will like. St. Paul, when instructing the Christian community at Ephesus, encouraged them to be authentic with one another: "[Put] away falsehood, speak the truth, each one to his neighbor, for we are members one of another" (Eph 4:25).

We don't want our friends to refuse to let us know the real version of who they are. If we don't want that in a friendship, we need to be aware of how authentic we are in our friendships. This helps us to grow in humility. Authentic friendships involve forgiveness when we do something wrong, honesty when the other hurts us or does something that we need to call out, and the ability to praise each other when praise is due. Healthy conflict is a part of every relationship, but authentic relationships weather those storms because the people involved practice humility. If we want our relationships to be lasting and life-giving, we need to be authentic.

VULNERABLE LEADERSHIP

Humble leaders can take organizations to the next level. Unfortunately, many leaders never fully grasp this. Instead of embracing humility, they create the persona of always being right, unapproachable, unquestionable. They want everyone to believe they are an expert in every area of the company. They aren't delegating their weaknesses; they are delegating their time. They want to do it all, but they don't have enough hours in the week to do all the work themselves. So they dole out work for other people to do, but they never really trust anybody else to do it as well as they do. They make sure that everyone knows their accomplishments and accolades. When they appear on the cover of a local magazine, the magazine shows up on everyone's desk.

This kind of leadership becomes ingrained in the company culture. What is valued is what you do, produce, and create on any given day. Competition is common, and collaboration sparse. Everyone wants to climb to the top.

You may not be a CEO or team leader at your workplace, but it's likely there are people who follow you. That makes you a leader in some arena. It may be that you are in charge of training the new administrative assistants. Maybe you are the leader in positivity within the office culture. If you are a parent, you are a leader in your family. You may be the person that takes charge in your group of friends.

How authentic are you in your leadership? How vulnerable do you allow yourself to be? Vulnerable and authentic leaders know a few things about themselves that they aren't afraid to share. They are willing to say that they aren't an expert in everything and that they delegate the tasks they are not good at to people more competent in those areas. They don't hold back in affirming and admiring those that have skills they lack. They share stories about times when they got things wrong. They apologize rather than shift blame. In short, they serve others.

Jesus spoke about this to his disciples as he prepared them to be leaders in the Church. He said, "You know that those who are recognized as rulers over the Gentiles lord it over them, and their great ones make their authority over them felt. But it shall not be so among you. Rather, whoever wishes to be great among you will be your servant; whoever wishes to be first among you will be the slave of all" (Mk 10:42–44).

This doesn't mean you are a pushover; it means you allow people to see that you are human rather than try to project the image of a perfect superhuman. People may feign respect for a leader who demands it, but authentic leaders earn respect.

Parents face this challenge in their leadership role with their children. You can make your kids obey you as a leader and head of the household, but what will happen when they are old enough to leave? Even before then, they will go through the motions of respecting your authority while looking for better ways to break the rules without getting caught. But children who genuinely respect their parents think twice about breaking the rules. (Yes, they still might break them—teenagers are wired to test boundaries.) How is this respect earned? By being authentic and vulnerable as parents—by being servant leaders. By getting down on one knee when necessary and saying, "I messed up today—do you forgive me?" Being authentic as a parent doesn't mean letting your kids walk all over you—but it does mean being honest about who you are.

CHASING AUTHENTICITY

Authenticity helps us recognize that we can't pretend forever to be someone we are not. The book of Proverbs tells us that this kind of deceit ultimately ends in ruin: "Whoever walks honestly walks securely, but one whose ways are crooked will fare badly" (10:9). Living authentically allows us to stop worrying about being esteemed and to stop fearing being wronged. We are confident in who we are before God, in our mind, and before others. Praying for authenticity is critical—and we do it by asking to become holy.

If we can't be authentic with others or ourselves, we won't be authentic with God. God really sees us, and if we desire to be who God created us to be—to be holy—then we must live authentically and pray for holiness. We ask for the grace to desire "that we may become as holy as we should." When we desire this, we start to live in the truth of who God says we are. We begin to want other people to see the real us—not some curated version of who we are. And because we know who we are, we let go of the dissonance we feel and experience the freedom that authenticity brings.

We can never fully let go of our desire to be esteemed, but we can recognize it and combat it by striving to live an authentic life. We do that by living in the truth of who God says we are, first. When we stand confident in his love, our desire to be esteemed is eclipsed by our desire to become as holy as God wants us to be—to be an authentic version of ourselves. Then we are comfortable with who we are and can, in patience, endure the one-sided three-hour conversation with a friend, the tense staff meeting where everyone is bent on justifying every aspect of their job, and the times when life dumps a bunch of water and a lemon slice on our lap and we wonder if anyone saw—and we can bear all those moments with humility.

Weekly Humility Practice

Look up one of the following scripture passages and choose one to write out on a notecard and place it where you will see it and read it at the beginning of every day: Psalm 139:13–16; Jeremiah 29:11; Romans 5:8; 1 John 4:19; Galatians 3:26; 2 Corinthians 6:18; and Romans 8:38. Remind yourself of the truth that God speaks about who you are.

Monthly Humility Practice

Take a friend out to coffee and listen more than you talk. Let your friend speak about him- or herself, and resist the urge to redirect the conversation toward yourself.

Yearly Humility Practice

Evaluate your leadership role, whatever that is. Ask your friends or spouse to name what they believe your core values are, and use their responses to evaluate your authenticity and humility. If you are a leader in a company, do a leadership assessment with people that work for you, gaining their feedback on your performance.

2.
GROWING
CONFIDENCE

From the desire of being preferred to others,
Deliver me, Jesus.
From the fear of being humiliated,
Deliver me, Jesus.
That others may be esteemed more than I,
Jesus, grant me the grace to desire it.

I couldn't stop staring at one comment. There were sixty on the page, but one cell of the spreadsheet kept calling out to me: "Way too scattered. Didn't get anything out of this. Least favorite."

I was reading feedback reviews from a recent speaking engagement. I always ask for the reviews because I want to improve as a speaker and as someone who preaches the Gospel. Most of the reviews I received were very positive—my average rating was 4.8 out of 5. If I were an Uber driver, that would be an amazing rating. If I were a restaurant on Yelp, that would put me in the top five restaurants in an area. That's a really good rating—but it wasn't a 5 out of 5 because of this one comment.

The person gave me a 1 out of 5, which is what you give someone when you really want to give them a zero but the system won't allow you to. Anyone giving a one-star rating knows what they are doing; they are unimpressed and restricted to a fixed rating system that doesn't allow them to fully demonstrate how unimpressed they are.

I should have focused on the fifty-nine positive ratings and comments, but I didn't. I just kept looking at that one. What could I have done differently to reach that one person, nay, that *one soul* better? I let that person down. I was the "least favorite." For that person, I was a waste of forty-five minutes.

It didn't matter to me that Jesus never had anywhere near a perfect approval rating. Many of the best restaurants, Uber drivers, politicians, doctors, whatever, don't have a five-star rating, but I wanted one for that conference and that single comment shattered me.

"I can't do this anymore, babe," I said to my wife as I collapsed onto my bed like a distraught Disney princess. The following dialogue ensued:

"There was one really bad comment. They all hated it," I said.

"All of them hated it? Who hated it?" my patient wife responded.

I looked up sadly from my crumpled-up pillow. "I don't know—this one person. It was an anonymous survey. I was only rated a 4.8 out of 5. I need to quit. I can't do this anymore." I sank back onto the pillow.

My wife laughed at me. Hard. Not the "laugh with you" kind of laughter, but the "you've got to be kidding" kind of laughter. But I wasn't. I was that dramatic. My confidence was totally blown by that one comment, and I really felt like I had nothing to offer anymore. As ridiculous as it sounds, this is probably a reaction we have all had at some time in our lives. When we receive negative feedback, at some point we've all done "critic's math." Jon Acuff, a leadership author and speaker, talks about critic's math in his book *Start*. He says, "1 insult + 1,000 compliments = 1 insult."

I use a slightly different formula for critic's math:

(Positive comments × 0) + (Negative comments × 100) = Your value

In my formula, all of my positive comments drop to zero and my negative comments are multiplied way more than they should be. In both formulas, we don't assign the correct weight to things. You might have your own version.

The correct formula for how we assess ourselves should look like this:

(Positive comments × 1) + (Negative comments × 1) = How people perceived your performance (not your worth) in a particular situation

That is a different kind of math. It is an honest assessment of how something went. Notice, too, what the formula tells us. Critic's math tells us what we are "worth," but the correct formula tells us only how we did in a particular instance—it doesn't determine our worth. Why do we use critic's math? What makes it so difficult to use an accurate formula when evaluating ourselves? It comes down to confidence.

WANTING TO BE WANTED

I've wrestled with confidence for as long as I can remember. I tried to combat my low self-esteem by looking for something on which I could place my worth—a firm foundation to stand on. Although my family was not wealthy, I grew up in an affluent area, and I thought that I would be more confident if I had money or dressed the way my friends dressed. As I got older, I spent my money on nice clothes but, alas, my confidence didn't increase.

I began to think that if I became really proficient at something, I would be confident. I could stand tall on my expertise. Unfortunately, the more I learned about something, the more I realized all I didn't know and all the opportunities I had to fail. Not only that, but I found that it was hard to determine if I was the best. That's why those surveys meant so much to me.

I wrote earlier that I valued those surveys because they helped me improve, and that is true. And it's also true that the real reason I looked at them was to validate my worth. I want to look at positive comments and be affirmed. I want to see how I am progressing in being popular, preferred, and an expert in something. When I see all positive comments, I feel like I'm getting there. When I see even one negative comment, I feel further away. I base my worth on whether people prefer me to others. Surveys are a great way to do that. They are also a great way to destroy our sense of self-worth.

That's why that one negative rating really stuck with me. It wasn't so much the score of 1 out of 5 (really a zero out of five), but the comment that I was *least favorite*.

There is an old song from the 1980s with the chorus, "I want you to want me," and I feel like that could be a mantra for my life. It plays underneath the ways I seek to be the preference of others. Preference is a subtle thing, and we don't talk much about it. There was a marketing campaign for Dos Equis beer that featured "the Most Interesting Man in the World," whose tagline was "I don't always drink beer, but when I do, I prefer Dos Equis." That was a brilliant marketing move: remind consumers of their desire to be interesting, preferred, and offer them a product to satisfy the desire.

Our preference says, "All things equal, this is the one I like the most. It is my favorite. It is the go-to." Preferences are more than momentary. We set our preferences in our phones and social media profiles. When something becomes a preference for us, it is something enduring. It even says something about who we are. When we know someone's coffee preference and get it for them without asking, that person thinks, "Wow, she got me a strong coffee with three creams, two sugars, and a wedge of lemon—just as I like it. She really knows me." Weird? Sure—but flattering? Absolutely.

Now, translate that into how you feel when you become someone's *preference.*

FROM THE DESIRE
OF BEING PREFERRED

The summer between junior high and high school I hung out with my friend Jon every day. We made it a thing. If either of us was going somewhere, we made sure the other was invited. We saw each other all one hundred days of summer break. We were each other's friend preference. Then we got to high school, and he started hanging out with sophomore friends. The day after we started freshman year, he and I never hung out again. His preferences changed. I was crushed.

It feels good to be preferred, and it gives us confidence. We think, "If that person likes me or if that group approves of me, then I'll have all the confidence I need." I remember hearing about some colleagues that were picked for an event instead of me, and I felt awful. The thought kept running through my mind, "Why wouldn't they want me? Why wasn't I a preference?" Just like when I received the negative review, I felt like giving up. After all, if I wasn't the number-one preference, what was I doing?

When I come across the petition "*From the desire of being preferred, deliver me, Jesus,*" in the Litany of Humility, my heart sinks. It is hard to give up being a preference. It hurt when I lost my best friend after that summer, and it stung when I was passed over for that event. I desire to be preferred because it gives me something worldly and tangible in which I can place my confidence.

Where do you draw your confidence? Is it from your job performance or a relationship? Where are you drawing your worth? If we are honest, we start to realize that our level of confidence fluctuates to some degree with our "approval rating." It is easy to be confident when people want you, but if that is taken away we find our level of confidence sinks rapidly. Our culture is a busy one, and we put a high emphasis on what we do and the value we bring to organizations, relationships, and even our community.

Individuals who are "high value" often appear more confident; after all, they are the ones worth the most.

Allowing our self-worth and confidence to hinge on the approval and opinion of others is a dangerous path. That is why our desire to be preferred is so detrimental to humility.

Confidence is key to humility. Read that again, because it is a principle that many people do not grasp. A distorted definition of humility equates confidence with pride and marks it as something to be avoided. But this isn't the case. Bravado and pride go together, but confidence is a requirement for humility. Only a person confident in her self-worth possesses the capacity to be humble. In the last chapter, we talked about where our worth comes from—it is a gift from God. We need to lean into that confidence because our desire to be preferred is tested when we face trials. The prophet Jeremiah said, "Blessed are those who trust in the LORD; the LORD will be their trust" (17:7). If we can't place our trust in Jesus and look to him as our source of self-worth and confidence, then we will look to our performance, the approval of others, or the ways in which others prefer us—which ultimately cannot support us when the storms of life arrive.

The litmus test for true confidence comes in how we face humiliation.

FROM THE FEAR
OF BEING HUMILIATED

Perhaps one of the most challenging lines in the Litany of Humility is the petition *"From the fear of being humiliated, deliver me, Jesus."*

Nobody likes to be humiliated. The time I forgot that I needed to make a presentation at a staff meeting and showed up totally unaware and unprepared is an experience I don't want to repeat. Sometimes we humiliate ourselves, other times humiliation is "done" to us—we are humiliated by somebody else.

Maybe a friend accidentally shares a personal secret when you are out with a group, or your date stands you up at a coffee shop. Humiliation can have a very negative connotation—we most often think of it when someone intentionally embarrasses us in order to do us harm.

The root of the word "humiliation" is the same as for "humble," and the literal definition of the word "humiliation" is "to make humble." Humiliation is designed to make people low.

Again, we need to clear up a misunderstanding of what it means to be humble. We may think that when we experience humiliation that we needed a correction of some sort, and sometimes that is true. Humiliating moments can teach us valuable lessons. I've never showed up to a meeting unprepared after that first (and only) time. We may walk into a competition overconfident only to be humiliated by our opponent. The history of sports is riddled with humiliating games where the underdog upsets the higher-ranking opponent. Other times, we experience humiliation not because we are overconfident or forgetful, but because of what someone does to us. These are moments we have no control over and are especially frustrating. But no matter how it comes about, we fear humiliation.

But we shouldn't. We don't have to like moments of humiliation, but we can't entirely avoid them. We can use those moments to either grow in confidence or to ask ourselves if our confidence has turned into pride. Humiliation orders the confidence necessary for humility.

BACK TO EARTH

In moments when we face humiliation because we were overconfident, the experience calls us back to the basics. Overconfidence actually reveals a lack of confidence. When a "superior" team loses to an underdog in an upset, it is often because the losing team strayed away from the basics of what made them successful. We say that they "forgot who they were." When we become overconfident, we place more value than we should in our gifts and talents rather than remembering that we are inherently valuable as children of God.

God gives us our gifts and talents to use for his glory, but he also expects us to develop and nurture them. We remember that, while we are loved, we also are human. We aren't superheroes. That mindset is humble—it isn't self-deprecating, but it prevents us from taking an easy route or becoming lazy.

People can become overconfident in relationships. They get married and then forget the basics of who they are as a spouse. They forget big events they once celebrated when they were dating. They stop saying, "I love you," or making an effort to spend time alone with their spouse. Why? Because they are overconfident in the relationship and place too much emphasis on the fact that they have been together for a long time or are bound by marriage, rather than remembering that relationships require continued work. Humiliation is not far off the moment your spouse, on the day of your anniversary, asks if you remember what day it is and you quizzically respond, "Tuesday?"

Humiliation helps us root our confidence in hard work rather than our past accomplishments. It keeps us grounded.

Our fear of public humiliation is the reason why even well-prepared people are often nervous before a business presentation. They are afraid of stumbling over their notes, saying the wrong thing, or tripping as they walk up to the podium. They don't want people to laugh at them, but more important, they don't want such incidents to diminish how they appear in the eyes of others.

This is what is at the root of our fear of humiliation—that we will look bad in the eyes of others. We fear that people will see us as human and flawed, not as a number-one preference. Once we are no longer preferred, we will lose our confidence. The humiliation is a double blow to confidence, but only if our confidence derives from the wrong thing.

IT GOT COLD IN MINNESOTA

One of the most humiliating moments I ever had occurred when I was asked to speak at an event in Minnesota several years ago. I was excited to be asked to give a presentation to a group of about four hundred students one evening. At the time, I was relatively new to booking events, so I made several mistakes. First, the event offered a very generous stipend, which I immediately refused. I asked for something lower. I felt like I wasn't worth the money they offered. Second, I spoke with the event organizer only once about the topic and thought I understood what he wanted. My wife was in her third trimester with our first child, so I was more focused on the soon-to-be-born baby than the event. As a result, I didn't ask the right questions of the youth minister. Then, in my pride, I didn't follow up to confirm content for the night. In my mind, I was such a gifted speaker that nothing could throw me off. I took another talk that I knew worked well with teenagers and tweaked it to fit the message. The only problem was that the talk didn't actually work with the message he wanted.

Nobody would have known that I prepared the wrong talk, except that as the event host introduced me he gave a three-minute overview of the talk that I was supposed to give. I listened, in horror, as he gave the big concepts of a talk that I had not prepared to a group of apathetic-looking Minnesota teenagers.

For the next forty-five minutes I fumbled through my talk, trying to connect the material I did prepare with what the talk was supposed to be about. It wasn't a glorious win; it was a horrific failure. I didn't even get the sympathetic "Hey, great job" comments you sometimes hear when you do something that was mediocre but people are too nice (especially in Minnesota) to tell you the truth.

It was humiliating. I sat through an awkward post-event dinner with several people that all wanted to avoid the atrocity of what had just happened. I am sure that they were happy I hadn't asked for the full stipend. When we first spoke, I basically told them I wasn't worth what they were willing to offer, and when I gave my talk I not only confirmed that sentiment, but perhaps made them regret they even paid me what they had. I went back to my hotel and collapsed into bed.

My problem, at the root of it all, was confidence. It began when I felt I wasn't worth the full stipend I was offered. My low self-esteem put an idea in my mind (and likely the mind of the event organizer) that I shouldn't have been the preference for speaking that night. To compensate, I became overconfident and misinterpreted what the event organizer wanted. I gravitated to a talk I was comfortable giving and didn't bother to clarify with the event organizer what the message should be. If I had run the talk outline by him, he would have told me that it was missing the mark. I worried that if I asked him to review the talk, he might think less of me and even regret hiring me. It was a perfect recipe for a moment of humiliation.

THAT OTHERS MAY BE ESTEEMED MORE THAN I

If we change our focus from being the preference of others to wanting others to be preferred, our fear of humiliation diminishes. The key to confidence is simple—we desire that others will be esteemed more than us. When we have that desire, we work because we love what we do, not to win praise. That brings freedom.

There is a simple logic here that we have all experienced but we rarely identify. Some of the most authentically confident people desire that others will be respected and esteemed more than they are. We say things like, "Whenever I talk to her, she makes me feel better about myself," or "There is something about his personality that just makes people better." Confidence doesn't need to prove itself. If we are confident in who we are and who God made us to be, we don't need to prove it. Additionally, we stop being afraid of humiliating moments because we know that they don't define us. If anything, they help us get better.

Growing in confidence really begins with desiring that others will be esteemed more than we are. The specific petition from the Litany of Humility is *"That others may be esteemed more than I, Jesus, grant me the grace to desire it."* The way we work toward this is to become promoters of others.

It may be easy to think that we need to first be confident before we can promote others, but it actually works both ways. Desiring that other people will be esteemed forces us to grow in confidence. When we put ourselves second in a conversation or promote another person's gifts and talents ahead of our own, we come to realize that it doesn't impact other people's view of us. The lie of preference is that people can only have one. We reason, "Well, if my best friend starts to prefer hanging out with someone else—if he starts to respect that person more— then I am going to be less." But this isn't true. We actually find the opposite is true. People don't lose respect for us, nor do we diminish our standing in the eyes of others—and that builds confidence. We realize that we are more than our accomplishments or our order of preference. In turn, we start to really live that out more. We start to desire that others will be respected even more than we are, and we actively work for that from a standpoint of confidence.

One of my favorite passages from the letter of St. Paul to the Romans sheds some light on how to grow in confidence and it contains very practical instructions for discipleship (12:9–21). One of my favorite lines is verse 10: "Love one another with mutual affection; anticipate one another in showing honor."

"Anticipate one another in showing honor" exposes the areas where we feel a tension between self-promotion in order to win esteem and promoting others so they are respected and preferred. I become less concerned about how I need to promote myself if I am confident that other people will give me the honor I am worthy of and, even if they don't, I am going to still honor them. It helps root out that source of pride in us but also has a profound impact on those that we honor.

BEING PROMOTED

When I began adjunct teaching at a university, I was ecstatic. I love to teach and was excited for an opportunity to do it at the college level. Adding to my enthusiasm was that the course I was teaching was online, and I think online learning is a great tool for students who can't be on campus. Since the school that was hiring me was on the other side of the country, I flew out to meet with the other faculty. I stayed with a friend of mine named Bob, who taught full-time at the school. He helped me get my paperwork set up, introduced me to the online learning department, and walked me through offices to introduce me to other professors.

What was incredible about the experience is that when he introduced me to other faculty, he told them that we designed the course I was teaching *together*. While it was true that I con-tributed some content to the online course, he had done much of the work. Why did he tell people we created the course together?

In his generosity, he wanted me to be esteemed as much as he was. I was a new faculty member, and he wanted the existing faculty to know that I had a place there. He knew that sharing his course with me would give me credibility. It took confidence for him to act this way. He knew his position on staff and was comfortable sharing it with me. He wasn't afraid that someone would say, "Wait, you needed to do this with another person? Wow, that really makes us think less of you." Nobody thought that. What did happen is that people respected me. It made me feel really good. We all love and appreciate moments like that. It also made me respect Bob even more than I already did.

Compare that experience with a time several years ago when I was working on a parish project. The person I was working with was well established and respected, but also busy. I did the majority of the work on the project, but when it came time to present it to the rest of the staff, my partner didn't mention me at all. In fact, he took credit for almost every piece of the project that I worked on—either explicitly (he said he did it) or implicitly (he didn't redirect back to me when he could have). At the end of the meeting, I felt terrible. I didn't even look like a sidekick on a project I worked hard on. I later learned this particular staff member struggled with confidence. He always felt he needed to earn his place, even though it was clear he was respected, preferred, and well liked. As a result, he never allowed anyone else to share that respect. He didn't use his platform to help others win esteem, even when they deserved it. Instead, he took the glory for himself. It was a moment I never forgot.

When we pray that others will be esteemed more than we are, we have to act like my friend Bob did. We can't be afraid that sharing the esteem we've gained will hurt us. The reality is that it won't—if anything, it only helps us grow in the eyes of others and worry about ourselves less.

Our desire to be preferred often makes us place our sense of confidence in what others think about us rather than in the knowledge that God loves us and defines our worth. If we seek our foundation in what others think about us, we are sure to sink. I know one saint who found that out the hard way.

WATER SKIING WITHOUT THE SKIS

The Gospel of Matthew has one of my favorite accounts of Jesus and his disciples. The disciples are on a boat during a windstorm, but Jesus was left on the shore praying. Suddenly, the disciples see Jesus walking on water. They don't believe it, and are terrified that they are seeing a ghost. Peter calls out to Jesus: "Lord, if it is you, command me to come to you on the water" (14:28). Jesus calls to Peter, and Peter steps out on the waves. As he walks, though, he suddenly fears the wind and waves and begins to sink. He cries out to Jesus to be saved, and the two make it safely back to the boat. When they arrive, the disciples worship Jesus.

We don't remember Peter's actions fondly in this narrative. Jesus himself admonishes Peter: "O you of little faith, why did you doubt?" (14:31). But I think much more is happening here; I think that this narrative provides an excellent example of what confident humility looks like with three practical steps for chasing humility, even in stormy water.

GET OUT OF THE BOAT

Peter is often cited for his lack of faith while walking on water, but let's go back to the beginning of Matthew's account. The disciples are terrified, but Peter calls out to Jesus. And Peter is the only one bold enough to actually step out onto the water. Remember, Peter says to Jesus, "If it is you, command me to come to you on the water." Peter does not know that the person on the water is really Jesus until the moment his feet touch the waves and he doesn't sink. If the disciples are actually seeing an apparition (and not Jesus), Peter is a dead man. That takes some confidence—but not confidence in himself; Peter has confidence in Jesus when he walks on the water.

Peter did something hard and took a risk, but had confidence that Jesus was going to sustain him. He trusted that Jesus wasn't going to let him fall.

We can relate this story to our own day-to-day lives. I wake up every morning at 5:00 a.m. to go work out. It isn't a fun thing, and when I first started this practice, it was terrible. I don't like waking up early. I would rather sink into the embrace of my warm bedsheets next to my wife than get up and put on workout clothes to go to the gym.

But a few weeks after I started this practice, I found that my days changed. I was more confident throughout the day and, not only that, I was more patient with others. I put less stock in my work performance and had better boundaries. By doing something good but difficult for myself, I learned that I could do hard things and that they were worth doing. That changed my whole perspective on the day. Maybe for you it isn't a morning workout, but an afternoon run. Maybe you get up to write five hundred words or to read thirty pages of a book. A daily ritual that is good for you but also challenging does two things: First, it is an investment of time into being a healthier person. That helps us grow in confidence. Second, it reminds us that we are capable of doing difficult things. I became a more self-confident person when I started waking up early and going to the gym.

KEEP YOUR EYES ON JESUS

It is likely that Peter got pretty far from the boat and fairly close to Jesus while walking on water. I used to think that Peter took a couple of steps out of the boat and sank, but there are some clues in the passage that this wasn't the case. First, Jesus was far enough away from the disciples that they couldn't tell if it was really him or a ghost (see Matthew 14:26). Second, Peter must have been closer to Jesus than the boat because when he began to sink he cried out, "Lord, save me!" and "immediately Jesus stretched out his hand and caught him" (14:30–31). Peter didn't yell for John to pull him out of the water or try to swim back to the boat. He must have been closer to Jesus—within an arm's length.

So what happened? Perhaps Peter became overconfident after walking all that way. Maybe he started to think that he was the one with the talent to walk on water, not Jesus. He took his eyes off the Lord and relied on his own power, but then Peter's attention focused on something else—the strong wind (Mt 14:30). He started to sink, and fear set in.

Perhaps Peter experienced humiliation. When he put more faith in his own abilities than in Jesus, he started to sink. We can sink, too. We will have moments when we encounter storms and strong wind. There will be times when life feels stacked against us. In those moments we can't rely on our own strength, and if we do, we are sure to experience humiliation. We are going to sink in the storm.

That's why we need to keep our eyes focused on Jesus, especially when things are going well. To avoid making Peter's mistake, stay rooted in prayer, daily. Make it a part of your routine, morning and night. Pray unceasingly, if you can (see 1 Thessalonians 5:17); it is the way we keep our eyes on Jesus and off of ourselves. When we pray regularly, even when we experience failure and humiliation, we won't sink. We will know who is keeping us above the water and where our worth comes from.

SHARE YOUR PLATFORM

After Peter's humiliating moment, he and Jesus walk back to the boat. That's a part of the story we don't usually consider. There is no other way they got back. What happens when they return?

"Those who were in the boat did [Jesus] homage, saying, 'Truly, you are the Son of God'" (Mt 14:33).

The disciples don't praise Peter. They don't comment on how incredible it was that Peter walked on water. They worship Jesus. They esteem Jesus more than Peter.

Of course, Jesus is God and deserves praise. Still, we have a model for what it looks like to share a platform—even if your platform is water.

When people think of a platform, they generally think of one claimed by a celebrity or a politician—people with influence and power. But each of us has a platform; we all have a group of people who respect us and whom we can influence. It might be a group of friends, our family, or our coworkers. If we really desire that other people be esteemed more than us, we have to be willing to share our platform with them. This is one way we "anticipate one another in showing honor." This requires being confident in who we are, beyond what we do; otherwise, we will guard our platform and keep it for ourselves.

Bob shared his platform as a full-time faculty member with me. Make it a point to share your platform with other people. Help give them credibility in your organization, group of friends, or with the people you influence.

The only way we can share our platform willingly is by remembering it isn't about us. Peter didn't seek praise when he got in the boat because he knew his worth in the eyes of Jesus. Peter was confident in God's love for him.

Weekly Humility Practice

Begin every day with a challenging morning ritual, and make prayer your foundation throughout the day.

Monthly Humility Practice

Find some way to promote the gifts of other people, even if it means promoting them over yourself.

Yearly Humility Practice

Evaluate your platform. Is there a way you could be helping other people or doing more with the influence you have?

3.
BEING GRATEFUL
FOR TODAY

From the desire of being honored,
Deliver me, Jesus.
From the fear of being calumniated,
Deliver me, Jesus.
That, in the opinion of the world,
others may increase and I may decrease,
Jesus, grant me the grace to desire it.

When I was a few weeks away from my high school graduation, I got a letter in the mail. It was a notice that I had received "one or more" scholarships for college. I was elated. I knew that paying for college, even a state school, was going to be no small task, and I didn't want to take out a lot of loans (spoiler alert—I took out a lot of loans). I knew that scholarships were the key to financial freedom after college. The night of the scholarship award event arrived, and I sat anxiously. I hoped for a big scholarship, even though I didn't apply for any. Maybe some benevolent donor had recognized my academic ability and high personal character and decided to give me a full-tuition scholarship. I wore a tie. My parents sat next to me. I waited.

They called my name for two awards. One was a $500 scholarship, which several students received, and the other was a $1,000 scholarship for students with financial need. I am embarrassed when I watch the video my mom has of me accepting the awards. I look like someone just told me my grandmother never loved me and that Santa Claus was a lie. I remember thinking, "If this is what I won, I don't even want it."

I WANT IT THAT WAY

I wish I could say that this was the first time my lack of gratitude surfaced, but I actually have a pretty solid record of throwing good things back in the faces of the people who give them to me. Like the Christmas when I didn't get the video game system I wanted, and I told my parents I would rather have them take back every gift they bought. It wasn't even about the system; I just wanted to tell my friends at school, after Christmas break, that I got that video game system. It didn't matter that, even after returning all my gifts, we could only afford the video game console and nothing else—no games, no controllers. I cried hard that Christmas.

At another point in my life I really wanted to work at a large parish with a big youth ministry program, and all my friends knew it. But when I was hired at the largest parish in our diocese with a potentially huge youth ministry program, all I did was complain to everyone about how it wasn't good enough.

I ran across an expression several years ago that summarizes my attitude really well: "I despise that which I have, and desire that which I have not." It is a fancy way of saying, "The grass is always greener on the other side." I find myself thinking, "If only I had this one thing . . . then I would be happy."

This attitude is particularly insidious when it comes to being honored. When we are honored, we win the award, we get the big thing, we advance in the eyes of the world. We think of honor a lot like we think of fame. Honor brings power. Honor brings money. When we are honored, we hold a status in the world that others don't enjoy. It is like an upgrade to first class.

FLY AWAY

I remember the first time my seat was upgraded on a flight; the experience changed my whole perspective on flying. For years, I was one of the people that boarded in Zone 10 and was forced to gate-check every piece of luggage I was carrying before uncomfortably walking to my middle seat near the back of the plane. Because of the layout of many planes, 95 percent of travelers have to walk by the first-class seats. It is an incredible tease. For a brief moment, you see what might have been: oversized seats with plenty of arm and leg room, a nice drink to sip while others fight for luggage space, and a relaxed, almost meditative mood. You think to yourself, these people are going to solve some big problems on this flight. They probably are executives or celebrities—or they saved up enough frequent-flier miles for this one glorious moment. Even the air smells better in that first-class cabin, but the moment is fleeting, and you are ushered toward the back of the plane next to a large man who chose to wear a cutoff T-shirt on this particular flight and a baby that smiles at you as you sit down as if to say, "I'm going to both cry and make the stinkiest diaper you've ever smelled about twenty minutes into this flight."

When I started flying more often, I achieved "elite status," which means a particular airline considered me a valuable customer. I learned that, as a perk, customers with elite status would sometimes be upgraded to first class. I recall the first time I was called up to the gate-agent desk in the airline terminal like it was a blissful dream. I was nervous at first, thinking, "What could possibly be wrong that they need to see me? Are they going to take all my bags again?" And then the gate agent spoke those enchanted words, "You've been upgraded." I swear tiny angels handed me my new boarding pass. I can only describe the flight as magical.

After that flight, it was hard to go back to sitting in the main cabin. I started to hope that I would be upgraded on every flight, and as I achieved higher ranks, my upgrades became more frequent. Pretty soon, I was upgraded on almost all of my flights. I boarded first. I got my drink. I looked with pity on those moving to the back of the plane as they passed by my plush, oversized seat. "Yes, fellow passengers, the air does smell better up here. Sorry, fellow passengers, but there is a large man with a cutoff T-shirt in seat 33A that is going to be your new best friend and a newborn in 33C that is superexcited to meet you," I thought.

To be honest, it is sometimes hard to enjoy first class because I worry about losing the privilege. My seat gets upgraded because the airline wants to keep my business buying those economy tickets. But the people sitting around me are wealthy, and some are celebrities. I once sat in the first-class cabin with all five members of '80s glam rock band Warrant. Unlike them, I don't belong there, and this recognition makes the experience less enjoyable.

Before I know it, the flight is over, and I haven't enjoyed anything. Status has a way of doing that. We never really appreciate where we are because we are too busy worrying about losing it or chasing the next thing. When you get to first class, you realize that what you thought was the top was actually somewhere in the middle, and you still have a long way to go.

FROM THE DESIRE
OF BEING HONORED

You may not struggle with the complex social dynamics of airplane seating, but I wonder if you sometimes struggle with looking at what you have and feeling like it isn't enough. We crave positions of honor, whether it is through airline status or some other special token. We've probably all known people who are not satisfied with a promotion because they have complaints about the new boss. It's likely that they will find fault with the board of directors if they reach top management. They will talk about how long the hours are and how thankless the job. They will confide in upper management that "everyone thinks they know how to do this job better—but nobody really knows how hard it is."

We strike at this disordered desire with the petition, *"From the desire of being honored, deliver me, Jesus."* Our desire for honor and status can hit us in all areas of our lives. Technology has made it possible for our social sphere to become digital. We judge our status based on how many followers we have or how many likes we receive on a given post. When I was a young teenager, life was all about how many friends you had and how popular you were. After I matured a bit, I was delighted to realize in college that life wasn't about being popular, but about being a good person. Then Facebook was introduced, and I signed up immediately, sending friend requests to any random person I could because it would make my network larger. So much for ditching the popularity contests!

It isn't enough to have followers, though; we need to know that they like us and "like" our posts. I have spoken to people that will take down a post if it doesn't receive the kind of response they want on a given platform. Bear in mind, I am not referring to companies that are managing a brand image—I am talking about individuals. But then again, social media has allowed everyone to cultivate a "brand," regardless of how authentic it might be. Social media has made it easy for people with no apparent skill set or major talent to become famous. It provides the illusion of honor with every new follower and each new liked post. Some people imagine what life will be like when a post of theirs goes viral.

Perhaps our distorted desire to be honored is most likely to shine through in the comparison we draw between what we have and what someone else has.

My wife and I discussed unfriending certain people on social media (or at least muting them so we didn't see their posts) because we tended to get jealous when we read or saw their posts. We found ourselves comparing our situation to theirs. She and I both know that social media is about as real as the relationships on *Jersey Shore*, but that didn't stop us from believing the lie. We instantly compared our day-to-day lives with a few pictures curated from the very best moments of a person's week, all shot with great poses and awesome lighting. On top of that, in the evenings we found that we were talking more about the lives of other people than our own. We would say things like, "Did you see what (insert name) posted today?"

Most of the time this wasn't gossip. We were talking about these posts as though they were the nightly news or a book we read. We usually didn't speak bad about the people who are posting—but we talked as though we spent time with them that day and learned this information in a private conversation.

We became jealous of what other people had, and in the process came to view the things we had as no longer good enough. Instead of being happy for the blessings in other people's lives, we got upset. Does this ever happen to you? My wife and I had to ask ourselves a tough question, and I'll pose the same question to you—why do we get jealous of what other people have, especially when it affects us in no way?

HEY, JEALOUSY

When my son was born, a lot of our friends didn't have kids yet, and we lived in a community where we once had some connections but had spent a few years away. We were living away from family, and as a result of these different factors very few people came to visit or offered us help. A couple that we knew from the parish made us a meal one night, as did our best friends (who lived in the apartment next to us). But that was it. No visitors, no meal trains, nobody volunteering to watch the baby so we could go grab a coffee for an hour. We took this in stride—until our friends next door started having kids.

It hurt more to see the outpouring of support our friends received with each new child than it did to not have had that same support. For a long time, my wife was angry and jealous. We got upset about the long meal train lists and visitors that were practically begging to babysit, even as we sat with a one-year-old that was adorable but at the same time soul-crushingly needy.

It's one thing to feel jealous, recognize it, and move on. But we didn't. We sat in our jealousy and let it consume us. There was no reason for that. The blessings of our friends had no bearing on our lives. They weren't taking things away from us. They weren't causing us harm. The way in which they were being honored in no way diminished or hurt our circumstances. So, why weren't we happier for them? Why were we unfollowing people on social media so we didn't see the good things they posted? The answer is simple—we weren't grateful for what we did have.

When we witness other people being honored in some way, we become jealous, and it makes us suspicious and ungrateful for what we have.

MORE MONEY, MORE PROBLEMS

When we desire honor, we become ladder climbers. Our desire is never satisfied because honor is fleeting. My airline status resets every year, and I fall back to the bottom of the ladder, only to begin the climb again. We win an award at one event but miss it the next. One day a celebrity is famous with a hit song, but a few weeks later nobody remembers who they are.

Honor is something we continually chase; we know it will go away, so we have to work for the next thing. I've read business and self-help books that praise this kind of unsatisfied attitude. Many people praised Steve Jobs for never being satisfied with Apple, his employees, or his success. But a lot of people also talk about how difficult Jobs was to work with and how caustic he could be to those he worked with when he felt they weren't measuring up.

Our desire for honor is never satisfied; we only want more because there is always a higher rung to climb. We look for the next upgrade, the bigger house, the better job, the greater influence. In the process, we end up jealous of what other people have because what we have is never enough. We get caught in this cycle, and it is hard to get out of. Gratitude is the key to escaping it.

FROM THE FEAR
OF BEING CALUMNIATED

As we have seen, with deliverance from any desire, a fear creeps in. As we pray against the desire for honor, we should also pray against the fear of calumny. In the Litany of Humility, the petition is, *"From the fear of being calumniated, deliver me, Jesus."*

If you are tempted to run to Google to find out exactly what this seemingly obsolete word, "calumniate," means, you aren't alone. I looked the word up when I first made this litany a regular practice. The simple synonym would be "gossip," but calumny is bigger. It isn't simply gossiping about someone; it is speaking about someone in a way designed to damage their reputation or hurt their social standing. Calumny is the opposite of honoring someone. When we are calumniated, someone is seeking to bring us down in the eyes of others. The worst part about calumny is that the statements are false—it isn't someone exposing us for wrongdoing or rebuking us. When we experience calumny, a person is intentionally attacking us using false information.

If you happen to run across the word today, you will likely see it in the context of a news story regarding a politician and probably during election season. It isn't just reserved for politicians, though. We can experience calumny in our close relationships or at work. Oftentimes, calumny stems from envy.

Gossip and calumny breed more of the same. In a toxic culture where people speak poorly about each other, we may find ourselves engaging in the same practice. I've encountered groups of friends and worked at various places where the standard practice is gossip and even calumny. I read once that Dave Ramsey, a popular author and financial adviser, docs not allow gossip at his company. It is one offense that is strongly reprimanded and even grounds for firing. Ramsey realizes how devastating calumny can be to the relationships in an organization. If we fear that someone is speaking poorly about us, it is likely that we are going to speak poorly about them. We engage in a war of words, but it is a cold war because we never actually face our opponent.

The destructive reality of gossip and calumny is highlighted throughout the Bible. Paul often warns communities against gossip as a major offense (see Romans 1:29-30; 2 Corinthians 12:20; Ephesians 4:29; and 1 Timothy 3:11, 5:13). Proverbs speaks about the impact of slander: "By a word the impious ruin their neighbors, but through their knowledge the just are rescued" (11:9).

SABOTAGE

Gossip can be especially devastating when it comes from leadership. I worked at an organization where the owner talked poorly about employees behind their backs. I hate to admit that if she was speaking to me about another employee, it actually felt kind of good. I felt like she trusted me enough to share that information and that I was for the moment in the inner circle. Oftentimes, other employees would pile on during the conversation. "Oh, he did that? Well, you will not believe what he did the other day during his shift." Sometimes the stories were totally false. After the conversation, though, we all couldn't help but wonder if the owner was also speaking poorly about us when we weren't around. Employees became so afraid of offending her that many stopped speaking up when they saw issues around the workplace that directly related to management. If someone else was slipping up, employees were sure to point it out—but if management made an error, everyone was silent. Eventually, the failure of management to inform us of a change in pricing resulted in my charging a friend a lower amount for a product than I should have. One day I learned that I had also been the subject of many behind-the-back conversations when I was told, unceremoniously, that I had been fired.

That unfortunate experience has remained with me. I sometimes wonder what my coworkers say about me behind my back and that anxiety is often fueled when I become envious of other employees as they are honored. I see someone get affirmed for a big project on a staff call but realize that my name isn't mentioned at all and I start to wonder if people are speaking poorly about me or even saying false things to upper management. Anytime someone seems short with me or sends me a one-word email I start to question if I did something wrong. I fear being calumniated, because I know that people could say something untrue about me that destroys what I've worked for.

YOU GET WHAT YOU GIVE

There are plenty of stories (unfortunately) about people that fell from grace because of what they did. What terrifies most of us is not being found out for bad things we did—many of us don't do horrific things—but rather having someone say false things about us that others believe and that we can't defend against.

When I was fired from the job I mentioned above, there was nothing I could say to convince management they made a mistake. I pleaded my case, and by the end of the conversation the tone had softened—to the point where the owner may have been ready to admit she was in the wrong—but it didn't change anything. If I had done something wrong, I could have accepted being fired, but I didn't. I left feeling ashamed over something I didn't do and frustrated because I knew that the other employees would be talking about me being fired for several weeks with no way for me to tell them what really happened.

That sort of fear can drive us to chase honor even more aggressively but also adds a new dimension as we seek to do it at the expense of others. The phrase "ladder climber" isn't used positively. It implies that an individual is willing to step over others so that he or she can move further up the corporate chain. This mentality can easily be deployed in behind-the-scenes warfare, as you look for opportunities to defame others while also promoting yourself. You are not satisfied with the current state of things but always want more. It is a hungry, destructive attitude.

We can fight this fear with gratitude. For years after I got fired (and still to this day sometimes) I get afraid when life seems too good. I feel uneasy and I start to wonder who is saying bad things about me and how it might impact me down the road. Do you know why I fear that? It isn't because I got fired—it is because I don't always speak well of people. I know that the words I speak don't always build up the honor of others, so why would I be so foolish as to expect others not to do the same to me? That is a serious symptom of pride—believing that you can speak poorly of other people but never have anyone speak ill of you.

Gratitude shifts the focus and takes power away from other people to determine your mood. God blesses us immensely, every day. How we choose to see and receive those blessings is up to us. When we become grateful and approach each day with a spirit of thanksgiving, we recognize that it is better to appreciate what we have rather than worry about a dumb thing someone might say about us. We stop worrying about the next big thing because we recognize that each moment is special and we really ought to live in it.

I'm coming to this realization with my kids. As a dad I feel a tremendous pressure to provide. When we had our first child, my wife really felt a call to stay home and raise him (and subsequently our daughter as well). The moment I became our sole source of income, I started to panic and poured myself into work. I justified it by saying that my wife was dedicating so much time to our kids that I needed to make sure I was providing. The transition to one income wasn't easy—we had a budget deficit every month, which I made up by traveling to speak and taking on extra projects apart from my full-time job. After a particularly long travel season, I looked at how much my son and (by that time) my daughter had grown and I felt a deep sadness. I was missing a lot of their growing up. Many parents travel and work demanding jobs, but it wasn't the long hours that were hurting my heart. It was the reality that I didn't appreciate the moments I did spend with my kids and my wife. Instead of simply relaxing, enjoying the present, and letting work go, I allowed projects and to-do lists to run in the back of my mind. I was there, but I wasn't present.

We need to live in the moment we have, right now, and be grateful for it. The practical path for that kind of gratitude is to allow ourselves to decrease.

THAT OTHERS MAY INCREASE AND I MAY DECREASE

The petition that addresses our need for gratitude is, *"That, in the opinion of the world, others may increase and I may decrease, Jesus, grant me the grace to desire it."*

This is a tough one to pray. On the surface, it seems like praying that you would hold the door for a person who gets in line in front of you . . . and then buys a $100 million winning lottery ticket right before you buy one. It is like asking to never take a vacation again but having to sit through slideshow presentations of your sister-in-law's most recent European adventure every Christmas.

If those things were in God's will and would help you grow in holiness, then yes, the petition definitely opens you up to them. But for most of us, it opens us up to real gratitude. When we begin a daily practice of gratitude, we start to see smaller things. We stop looking for the big moments that we count as blessings, and we look for the little ones. Our pursuit of ladder climbing and the endless endeavor of earning honor cease. Instead, we are thankful for the food we eat, the jobs we have, the air we breathe, and precious moments with our family. We realize that true increase lies in the love we give and receive, not in the likes and followers we get. It is the opposite of the worldly view of increase, which is why the words "in the opinion of the world" matter so much. God does not want to take good things away from you. On the contrary, God wants to increase the good things in your life. They just aren't the things that the world sees as "increase." The good things God wants to increase in your life are things that will lead you to be a holier person; that means a decrease in things that would distract you—including material possessions.

NOTHING COMPARES TO YOU

The words "he must increase; I must decrease" were spoken by John the Baptist, the last prophet before Jesus (Jn 3:30). He was a wild man and lived and preached in the desert, yet many came to hear him. The life of John the Baptist gives us a radical example of someone who let go of the desire of being honored and the fear of being calumniated, and who grasped hold of gratitude.

John the Baptist was Jesus' cousin. The two may have grown up together, but John went into public ministry first. John's whole life centered on paving the way for his younger cousin. His only goal was that Jesus would be praised and honored. People talked poorly of John, but it didn't deter his mission. When asked about the Messiah, he tells people that "one mightier than I is coming after me. I am not worthy to untie the thongs of his sandals" (Mk 1:7).

Imagine the elation John had when he is asked to baptize Jesus. When John was on the brink of imprisonment and ultimately death, he expressed his joy and gratitude in seeing Jesus' manifestation as the Messiah: "So this joy of mine has been made complete. He must increase; I must decrease" (Jn 3:29–30). John was grateful to be a part of Jesus' early ministry, and now he was ready to step back.

In a contemporary context, people might have thought John crazy. He had a following, a large ministry, and high levels of influence. Why give up? Why not compete with the ministry of Jesus or at least join forces? John even sent disciples away from him to follow Jesus instead (see John 1:35–37). John sought to become small so that love for Christ would increase instead.

THIS IS HOW WE DO IT

There are some simple practices that will help us cultivate gratitude and, in the process, lessen our desire to be honored and our fear of being calumniated.

Make time every day to reflect on what you are grateful for. God presents us with incredible blessings, and every gift comes from him. One good practice is to keep a blessings journal. At the end of every day, take a moment to write down three areas for which you are grateful. Offer a prayer of thanksgiving.

A physical journal or notebook is good for a couple of reasons. First, our brains remember information differently when we write it longhand rather than type it. While a digital journal might be convenient, our brains don't process the information we are recording in the same way. Second, you can look back on the pages of your blessings journal in difficult seasons and remember that God has blessed you and will continue to be faithful. This kind of remembrance is important. Scriptural figures such as Moses and King David and great spiritual writers such as St. Ignatius advocated the importance of recalling the good things God has done when times are dark.

Express gratitude often and gratuitously. I make it a point to look service professionals like wait staff, flight attendants, and store clerks in the eyes and say "thank you." I even use their names if they are wearing a nametag. Many people don't think to do this. If you want to conduct a unique social experiment, sit in a coffee shop near the cash register and observe how many people express gratitude for the service they are provided. I've spoken with people that argue, "Well, it is their job. You shouldn't need to be thanked for something you are supposed to do." I disagree. Expressing thanks is an important part of our human interactions. Even if someone has to do something, we should thank them.

Gratitude also does something for us. Saying thank you is a small way of acknowledging that what is happening is a blessing—that someone is helping you. Express gratitude to your spouse and your friends often. Marriage ends up on rocky ground when we begin to take our spouse for granted. A simple word of thanks can go a long way. The same is true for those in leadership positions in the workplace. We may take for granted that people know we appreciate their hard work. Gratitude helps us to focus outward rather than inward.

Finally, receive the gratitude of others well. How often do you refuse someone when they thank you? You may not even realize you are doing it. I know many people who respond to thanks with, "Oh, it's no big deal," "You don't have to thank me," or "No problem." Those are subtle ways of refusing thanks. The way to respond to "thank you" is simple—you say, "You're welcome."

Our desire for honor puts us in a dangerous cycle of ladder climbing, suspicion, and gossip. To break out of the cycle, we must cultivate gratitude and work so that "others may increase" while focusing on the small blessings of our daily lives and routines. Gratitude is a key aspect of humility, and those that live it well find freedom that the cycle of honor chasing can never bring.

Weekly Humility Practice

Get in the habit of expressing gratitude often, and start a daily blessings journal. Take a few moments after writing to thank God for the particular blessings you experienced.

Monthly Humility Practice

Handwrite a letter of gratitude to someone you want to thank.
Make the letter about them, not you.

Yearly Humility Practice

Do something that honors another person in a big way. It could
be your spouse, a coworker, or a friend. It could be on their
birthday or another special occasion, but make it something
that feels over-the-top and gives them a sense of increase while
you remain behind the scenes.

4.
LOVING OTHERS

From the desire of being loved,
Deliver me, Jesus.
From the fear of being despised,
Deliver me, Jesus.
That others may be loved more than I,
Jesus, grant me the grace to desire it.

I remember when I fell in love for the first time. I was a freshman in high school and was dating Rebekah. We were close friends before we started dating and, as a freshman, I thought that our love story was pretty great. I told her that I loved her about a month into the relationship. I gave her roses and wrote her a poem. I loved the way I felt when I was with her. I loved how she made me a better person. I loved that I had someone I could call when I was happy, hurting, frustrated, or excited. She loved all those things about me, too. But our love was cut short because love isn't a long-term situation when you are ninth-graders.

We broke up a few months into our junior year of high school. I told her that she only loved me because of how I made her feel—that she didn't love me for me. I feel terrible writing that because I loved her for selfish reasons, too.

As it turns out, we didn't really love each other at all.

We use the word "love" in a lot of different ways. There is this place I love to go to in Philadelphia called Monk's Café. The mussels they serve there are second to none. I love them, but I don't *love* them.

I am a big fan of the Green Bay Packers. As a Wisconsin native, I grew up watching games with my dad. Then I went through a weird hipster phase in college when I thought football was overrated, but then as a young adult I really got into NFL football and the Packers again. I tell people I love the Packers. I mean, I love them, but I don't *love* them.

I love visiting Flagstaff, Arizona, in the winter with my family, but I don't *love* it.

I love peanut butter M&Ms and watching *Forrest Gump*, but I don't *love* those things.

I love to use the word "love," but I feel like I've watered down the meaning.

I'm not the only one diluting the meaning of the word, though. We've all, in some way, distorted the meaning of love, and sometimes it can be difficult to know what love actually is.

FROM THE DESIRE
OF BEING LOVED

We are wired for love. As Christians, we know that love is the whole purpose of our creation. We were created to know, love, and serve God, and to love and serve each other. Our capacity for love is less than what God, who is love, offers—but he seeks to stretch our human heart. That can be uncomfortable, so we seek to fill our desire to be loved in other ways that are more comfortable.

The most critical petition in the Litany of Humility, and probably the hinge point of the whole prayer, is, *"From the desire of being loved, deliver me, Jesus."* Of all the petitions, this is the most frightening.

There are probably few people that can pray these words without feeling uneasy. We all want to be loved, and our desire for love isn't a bad thing—but it can easily be distorted. In fact, because it is our motivating desire and the reason that we were created, it is always a prime target for the devil. If we chase a false idea of love, we do not realize we have a need for authentic love that will actually bring fulfillment in our lives.

USING LOVE

Distortions of love come in many forms in our culture, but the most common one that we experience is exemplified by my relationship with Rebekah. We thought we were in love, but we were both in the relationship for selfish reasons. We loved the other person only as much as they made us feel good about ourselves. This isn't a high school mistake; many people think that love is something they feel, and ultimately that feeling is self-centered. We talk about what the other person can do for us, and that brings loaded expectations. We want our partner to bring us happiness, a sense of fulfillment, and companionship through life's ups and downs. We want our loved one to support us. When we find someone who does these things, we think we have found love.

Because we think we've arrived at real love, we do our best to reciprocate the support, affirmation, sense of fulfillment, and happiness. But our motivations may be flawed. We may love that other person just because we want to receive love in return. Love becomes a transaction. It is the relational currency we exchange in order to feel good about who we are. With this mentality, it is no wonder so many marriages end after a few years. As I grew through my young adult years, I went through the normal phase of "wedding season" where many of my friends got married. What I didn't realize was that my postmodern young adult life cycle would also include a "divorce season." This wasn't celebrated but was talked about in quieter tones or via text messages as people stopped posting pictures of their spouse on social media until it was confirmed that they were separated.

If we view love as a contractual agreement, then it is no wonder that so many people treat marriage as something that can be broken, like a contract with a buyout clause. Of course, there are legitimate reasons why a couple may choose to separate; it may not involve a misunderstanding of love. But when two people view each other as the missing piece that they needed in order to feel whole, disaster isn't far. No person, regardless of how amazing they are, can ever fulfill us. When we look to another person for that, ultimately we are disappointed.

Our desire to be loved can lead us to use another person, and it can also lead us to be used by others. It is heartbreaking to think of all the ways the words "I love you" have been used to justify the abuse and harm of another person. Why are those words so powerful even in the midst of abuse? Because we were created for love, so we settle for a distortion or imitation of it so long as we can convince ourselves it is the real thing. If we haven't experienced authentic love, then this settling is much easier. It is living up to the standard we've been given, which on a divine scale is woefully deficient.

Our desire to seek love is ingrained in us from our creation, but the thought of letting go of our distorted views of love will be met with fear. Remember, if love is our greatest longing, then the devil uses that longing to tempt us to an imitation that cannot satisfy. This temptation is amplified by fear—a fear that we will be despised rather than loved.

FROM THE FEAR
OF BEING DESPISED

The moments when I've encountered someone who truly did not like me—to the point where I would say that person actually despised me—are few, but very real. When I think about those moments, praying the petition, *"From the fear of being despised, deliver me, Jesus,"* takes on a whole new meaning.

A few years ago, an individual started attacking me anonymously via social media. This person created a fake account and targeted me and a few other people with insults, provoking messages, and anger. I ignored most of it as noise, but the messages got angrier and more focused—ultimately ending with the account being suspended for its vile content. I have no idea who the person was, but I am certain they despised me. I'm not really sure why.

From what I could tell, this person knew me only from my public ministry and perhaps had seen me speak. They probably never met me in person, but they hated me. I tried to let it all go, but it still makes me uncomfortable. There is someone out there who hates me enough to make a fake account and use it to attack me personally, and I have no clue who they are.

We don't want to be despised by someone anonymous, and we definitely don't want to be despised by people that are close to us or that we care for. This is where love gets twisted. When we want to be loved and not despised, it can be difficult to make the right decisions. Sometimes in a relationship we need to speak hard truths, end the association, or even rebuke and correct someone. There is a risk in those moments that a person will quickly go from loving us to despising us. Some people deal with this tension by never calling another person out, even when they should, or by continually giving in and violating their own moral code. The fear of being despised is powerful.

What is the cure for this? How do we find authentic love? Do we understand it enough to seek it? The key to this part of the Litany of Humility, and to living humility, is understanding what it means to love our neighbor as ourselves. If we don't really know what authentic love is, then we won't really understand what it means to love our neighbor.

THAT OTHERS MAY BE
LOVED MORE THAN I

When I was a child, a tiny crucifix hung in my room. My mother put it there near my light switch. I asked her about it at various times, and she always responded that it was there to protect me. Of course, what she was teaching me was that Jesus was always there to protect me. The physical crucifix served as a reminder of God's protection and providence. That crucifix is a sign for millions of people of God's protection, providence, and, most important, God's love. Perhaps you have a cross hanging in your home. The reality of the Cross is bigger than decoration—it shows the lengths to which God is willing to go for us. It signifies what authentic love is. We might take this for granted. Many people know that a crucifix represents God's love, but we don't meditate on this beautiful truth as much as we should. St. Paul says that the Cross proves God's love for us, because Jesus died for our sins while we were sinners (see Romans 5:8). Jesus did this freely and we can accept or reject it, but we don't do anything to earn it.

St. Paul had this kind of love in mind—a self-sacrificial, divine love—when he wrote his famous lines "Love is patient, love is kind" (1 Cor 13:4). We hear these words proclaimed at weddings and maybe even have them framed on our walls, but something is lost in the translation of "love." We fall back on our distorted images of love, and though some of those images may be good, they don't measure up to what St. Paul had in mind.

The word St. Paul used, in Greek, was *agape*. It was one of several Greek words for love. Recognizing that love can refer to a variety of things, the Greeks constructed a few different words for what we translate simply as "love." Agape is the highest form of love, a concept largely of theology and philosophy because it seems unattainable by human standards. St. Paul sees in Christ this great love—a love that is embodied in self-sacrifice. This kind of love is not selfish or self-seeking. It is patient and desires the good of the other person.

Many people view love as a fixed commodity. If someone else is being loved, we reason that we are loved less. In this conception, we seem capable of running out of love. All that is left, then, is the opposite emotion—being despised. Being despised isn't simply being hated; it is being rejected. To avoid being despised, we want to make people love us (or at least like us). In the process, things become more about ourselves than the other person. Receiving love is about us not feeling rejected, hated, or alone. Just as we can engage in critic's math, we can develop a warped economy of love where if we are loved more than we are disliked or despised or ignored, then those moments when we feel rejected will sting less. Maybe we could forget about those situations of rejection altogether. But we don't. Since this idea of love involves us getting love rather than giving it, it doesn't matter how many people love us; the rejections of others still hurt. We wonder, "Why can't I get that one person to like me?"

The remedy for our distorted desire to be loved and our fear of being despised is found in this petition from the Litany of Humility: *"That others may be loved more than I . . . Jesus, grant me the grace to desire it."* When we pray for this grace, we trust that Jesus provides it, and then we need to take the next step. We need to embody love.

BECOMING LOVE

If we want to know authentic love, we need to return to the Cross of Christ. We are called to love others with agape love—the self-sacrificial love that Jesus models for us. This petition in the Litany of Humility requires something of us—that we not simply pray but also act. There is a fear when we begin to love others in the way Jesus calls us to love them. We know, especially when reflecting on the Cross, that authentic love brings suffering but also resurrection. When we love someone, we open ourselves up to pain but also joy. We live the sacred pattern of the Paschal Mystery when we love other people. Love requires a willingness to die to one's present reality in order to find new life in loving another.

When I met my wife and began to fall in love with her, I was presented with a choice. If I really wanted to love her, I needed to open myself up to sharing her reality. That meant that I would change; in some ways, I would need to die in order to experience the fullness of love. I would need to accept a new life. But that meant I would get to know all the joy that truly loving another brings. I would experience companionship, emotional intimacy, and the happiness that comes with making new memories with someone. But love doesn't bring only those things. In sharing her reality, I also opened myself up to pain. I would need to share her burdens, and hurt when she hurt. If I really wanted to love her, I couldn't just open myself up to joy while shutting the door on pain.

When we married, we made that choice more deeply. When we had our first child, love grew and opened the potential for new joy but also for new pain. Now there was a third person that could experience joy and pain, and I had to choose to love him and share that reality, or become a distant father and avoid it.

The only way to avoid the suffering and inevitable death that love brings is to avoid loving. The reality and promise of the Cross remind us, though, that suffering and death are not the end. Beyond the dying there is new life.

This theology of love makes sense within our deepest relationships, but it also is the necessary way to love our neighbor in humility. The love that we have for our neighbor varies in degree but not kind. In our marriages, families, and lifelong friendships, love looks different and achieves a degree of intimacy only appropriate for those deep relationships. To others, including our enemies, we extend the same kind of love but to a different degree.

COMPASSION AND MERCY

The virtues by which we extend love to our neighbors are compassion and mercy. Compassion is different from empathy, but many people confuse the two. When we feel empathy for another person, we see the world from their perspective and gain a better understanding of what they are feeling. Empathy is an important skill, but it isn't the same as compassion.

"Compassion" literally means "to suffer with." When we feel compassion for another person, we don't empathize with them; we feel what they are feeling. We suffer alongside them. St. Paul talks about this ability to feel the suffering of another in his first letter to the Corinthians. He uses the analogy of a body to talk about how interconnected we all are in Christ. He says, "If one part suffers, all the parts suffer" (1 Cor 12:26). Many of the greatest world leaders understood this reality. Some saints felt this so acutely that they realized they could never be really happy so long as suffering existed in the world. We can feel empathy for a person by losing our self-centered attitude, but we cannot love someone unless we show them compassion.

Mercy and sympathy are similarly confused. When we feel sympathy, we feel sorrow for the circumstances of another person. That sorrow can turn into compassion, but it can also turn into pity. Pity represents a disconnect from compassion; instead of feeling sorrow *with* someone, we feel sorrow *for* someone. That word, "pity," immediately evokes a certain kind of image in our minds. It is an image of power—one person is looking down on another from above and feeling bad. We think of someone who is rich feeling pity for someone who is poor. Mercy also involves power, but it doesn't involve pity. When we feel pity, we look down from above. When we wish to extend mercy, we kneel alongside in order to raise up.

God's love is always experienced as mercy. We don't do anything to deserve or earn God's love, yet he chose to come alongside us by becoming incarnate. Jesus Christ, the second person of the Trinity, humbled himself and took on human flesh as an act of love—which we experience as mercy. We are called to imitate that kind of humility. When we show love, we are often called to show it as mercy.

Mercy involves a disparity of power. One common realm where we experience mercy is in the act of forgiveness. When someone forgives us, they are extending us mercy. They hold the power to keep us bound up in our fault or to release us by their forgiveness. Have you ever asked someone to forgive you and that person told you they couldn't? A friend once told me he could never forgive me for accidentally tripping him when we were on the playground. He ripped his new khakis and was so upset. I felt terrible all day.

The next day at school, he acted as though nothing had happened, and things went back to normal. But I remember the awful feeling of not being forgiven. We've all had petty disputes like that as kids, but they can continue even as adults. Sometimes a relationship becomes so fractured that forgiveness is impossible. When someone looks at us and refuses to forgive, we become trapped in a way. They hold power over us.

We recognize that sense of power when we are on the other end. When I was fired from that job I mentioned earlier, I refused to forgive the owners. When I got dumped in college by my long-term girlfriend, I spent a lot of time being angry and not forgiving her for the way that it all happened. I refused to offer mercy. It made me feel self-righteous. It made me feel vindicated. It made me feel strong. When we hold the power to forgive someone or to keep them trapped in a fault, it can bolster our pride in some really ugly ways.

What I realized after several years of bitterly holding on to these wrongs was that I was the one trapped. That's why it is so critical to show mercy and why it is key to humility. When we refuse to forgive our neighbor, we feed our pride on the sense of power that our refusal gives us. Eventually, people move on whether we forgive them or not, but we stay stuck in the angry, bitter prison we build for ourselves. We proudly hold on to the wrongs committed against us for years, smug that we were right and they were wrong.

How many people are trapped in that kind of anger due to a family argument or an online conversation? Maybe you are trapped in it, right now. Mercy frees us—even if the people that we need to extend that mercy toward are no longer in relationship with us or are not in a place where we can contact them. In that case, mercy is simply letting it go and forgiving them in our hearts—regardless of whether we can express it to them.

Sometimes showing mercy isn't about a broken relationship, but about addressing the disparity of power and resources that we know exists. When we see poverty, we need to address it with compassion and empathy. Loving people in that situation can be uncomfortable. It is easier to ignore poverty than to rectify it and feel the suffering that comes from it. The same is true for marginalized groups or individuals that are the subject of discrimination. We can turn away from injustice in order to remain comfortable, but that isn't really loving our neighbors. Compassion and mercy make us humble—compassion because it lets go of our own self-interest; mercy because it requires we step down from a position of power in order to meet another.

THE STORY OF THE GOOD SAMARITAN

We can learn much about compassion and mercy, and therefore love, from a well-known parable. When Jesus is asked about the greatest commandment, he responds that we should love God and love our neighbor (see Luke 10:25–28). But the person who asked the question presses Jesus: "Who is my neighbor?" (v. 29). The person asking is a "scholar of the law," which is probably why Jesus responds the way that he does.

Jesus tells a story about a man going on a journey, who is attacked and robbed along the way. He is left for dead. A priest walks by, but passes the beaten man on the other side of the road. A Levite does the same thing. Finally, a Samaritan sees the beaten man and "was moved with compassion at the sight" (Lk 10:33). He cleans and bandages the man's wounds, puts him on the animal he was riding, and takes him to an inn, paying for the man to stay there until he recovers.

I imagine the scholar of the law that asked Jesus "Who is my neighbor?" must have been in shock. Samaritans and Jews were not friends. They existed in a tense relationship because they disagreed on big things. They didn't associate with each other, and they worshipped in different places. We know that the man who was robbed is a Jewish man, not a Samaritan, because he is traveling from Jerusalem, the Jewish center of worship. He is passed by two of his own people—priestly people, no less—who avoid him, probably because touching the blood of the beaten man would have made the priest and the Levite ritually unclean.

But the Samaritan, an enemy, is moved with compassion. He suffers with the beaten man. He goes way beyond expectations for someone who is part of a broken relationship between two different peoples.

The story served its purpose in answering the question, "Who is my neighbor?" but Jesus asks the legal scholar, "Which of these three, in your opinion, was neighbor to the robbers' victim?" (Lk 10:36). The scholar of the law begrudgingly admits, "The one who treated him with mercy." A disparity of power existed, but love was shown. Jesus drops the mic with his final words to the scholar, "Go and do likewise" (v. 37).

LOVE DOES

When we pray the petition *"that others may be loved more than I,"* we are given the grace to be that love, to follow Jesus' command to "go and do likewise." We can practice loving others more than we are loved by focusing on four intentional areas:

- love of self,

- vocational love,
- compassion for our neighbor,
- mercy for the other.

Love of Self. While this may seem counterintuitive and prideful, if we rightly understand what love of self means, we recognize that it is a necessary step in loving others. It is easy to forget that the second great commandment that Jesus preaches is to "love . . . your neighbor as yourself" (Lk 10:27). We crudely translate this as the Golden Rule, to "do unto others as you would have them do unto you," but this commandment goes much deeper.

We love our neighbors as we want to be loved ourselves and as we have been loved by God. An authentic love of self doesn't come from pride but from recognizing our great worth in the eyes of God and the price he paid to ransom us from death. In short—God loves you and me immensely. If we have received that love, then we must also view ourselves with dignity and worth. That is authentic love of self. When we possess that, we can recognize that our desire to be loved is fulfilled in God, who loves us infinitely. We will then turn that desire outward and seek to share that kind of love with others.

Vocational Love. Our vocation is God's calling for us. Some say that it is God's plan for us. If you are married, your vocational calling is marriage. If you are a priest or religious brother or sister, your vocational calling is one of service to the Church and the people of God. All people are called to holiness, so if you are currently single, your vocational calling is to love those around you well and seek to grow in relationship with God. The people connected to us through our vocation receive the highest degree of our love. It would be disordered if a husband loved his friends to a higher degree than his wife and children, yet we know this situation isn't uncommon. We also know how problematic it becomes. Those closest to us are the ones we offer our most self-sacrificial love. They are the people we open ourselves up to suffer alongside.

As you seek to grow in vocational love, ask yourself how you can be more selfless. Do an act of service for those you are close to that you wouldn't normally do. Be mindful of the words you use with these people, and build them up. Do something just because and make yourself emotionally available, not just physically present.

Compassion for Our Neighbor. We are becoming more calloused as a culture as the needs of others are perhaps heard but not addressed. Information is more available than ever, and through social media the challenges of discrimination, harassment, violence, and disease are put on public display. Advocacy campaigns promise action, but it seems as though little is done. Our exposure to all of this information has the potential to make us more compassionate, but that is certainly not always the case. In fact, many of us are becoming apathetic. We are accustomed to hearing about tragedies and are beginning to simply accept the current climate as the way things will always be. We must shake off our apathy and embrace compassion, but to do so means we open ourselves up to the suffering of others and walk with them. Their pain becomes our pain.

Acts of service, especially ones that stretch us, are humbling ways to practice compassion. I served teenagers for many years as a youth minister, and part of that ministry involved sponsoring service projects. I quickly learned that teens gravitated to the projects that made them feel good. For some it was working with homeless individuals, and for others it was spending time at a daycare. I've learned that teenagers and adults are not so different. When we choose to serve, it is often more about us than those that we serve. This isn't to say that it is wrong to feel good about serving others, but that should not be the only reason we do it. If service is all about how we appear before others and how it makes us feel, we can quickly develop a hero complex—believing that we are the savior of those we serve—and then fall right back into our desire to be loved. We want those we serve to love us, thank us, fall over themselves to tell us how needed we are.

Compassionate service is rewarding because we participate in an exchange. We feel what another feels, and rather than taking pity on them or simply viewing the world through their lens, we become a part of their world. It might mean we never get any thanks, or those we serve might not know that we serve them. It might mean dropping an area of service that has become routine and starting one that makes us uncomfortable for a while, just so we can realign our priorities and our hearts. Eventually, compassion becomes the natural response in these relationships of service. We walk *with* others, rather than in front.

Mercy for the Other. A friend of mine once put a riddle to a priest. She said, "If Jesus says that there is no greater love than to lay down your life for a friend, but also says we need to love our enemies, does that mean that there is really no greater love than to lay down our life for our enemy?" The priest, who was wise, responded with the simple statement, "If you really loved your enemy, he wouldn't be your enemy anymore." It is true that we can't do anything about how people feel about us. We can't control the hearts of other people. But we can control our hearts. We all make enemies, but we don't necessarily call them enemies. We simply look at them as "the other." The person or group that is not *us* becomes our opposition and our enemy—the person with differing political views, the coworker that seems to be negatively impacting our projects, the individual that puts forward an opinion we don't like. Again, social media has made it easier than ever to create enemies out of the other.

A friend of mine posted a video on his social media page of a woman being interviewed. The viewpoint she expressed was one I agreed with, though she didn't articulate it well and the interviewer (who had already labeled her as an enemy) provoked and pushed, rendering the woman inarticulate and flustered. The interviewer proceeded to mock her until the segment was over. I was surprised at how many of the comments on the post came from practicing Christians fueled by anger. They called her stupid and several other things that I do not want to record. I decided to try an experiment. I knew that I could explain this viewpoint better than was done in the video, so I posted a comment offering an opportunity for people to enter a dialogue with me, in hopes they would see the woman's point of view and maybe find they were closer to agreement with her than they realized. Nobody took me up on my offer. Not one person. But several people continued to leave angry comments long after I had left mine. They weren't interested in learning; they had found an enemy and wanted to attack.

People lament the growing political divide in our world, but the divide is not between political parties or politicians but between us and *the others*.

This is nothing new. All racism, sexism, and other unjust forms of discrimination start that way. I've heard people speak in cruel terms about those in poverty—they've made them the other. When someone is the other, they don't get our love, because they are the enemy. We don't show mercy to the enemy for fear that it would be seen as weakness.

We must eliminate the mentality of "the other" and simply embrace "the us." That doesn't mean we whitewash the challenges presented in our relationships. It doesn't mean that we erase history or overlook areas in need of healing. It does mean that we stop seeing people that stand in opposition to us as inhuman monsters incapable of dialogue and unworthy of our love. It means that we stop looking at those that are on the margins, are discriminated against, and are ignored as separate from us and somehow undeserving of mercy and compassion, and instead enter into their world. When we step into that world, sometimes we must speak, sometimes listen, and other times just sit in silence as a companion.

This is why the story of the Good Samaritan is so powerful for our day. It is a story of real love of neighbor, even when our neighbor is the other. It isn't a bare minimum of compassion, either, but mercy that goes above and beyond what is expected.

Who is the other in your life? Who have you labeled as the enemy? Your failure to love that person or group of people is your biggest stumbling block to humility. Hatred is a form of pride, because it makes us judge and executioner in our minds. Who are we to hate someone when our God forgives us? Who are we to determine the dignity of another person when our God has created us with immeasurable worth? A response of mercy requires humility, as does the reception of mercy from others when we need it.

We cannot really live humility in a way that impacts other people until we accept the reality that we must give the love that we want to receive, while expecting nothing in return and being content in the love that God gives us. We don't need to perfect this attitude or even be far along the road; we just need to recognize it. Humility is a progression, but learning to love well is critical in the movement from internal humility to external humility and service of others. Our internal humility will transform us, but our external humility will radically transform our world and those around us.

We all want to be loved, but we first must receive the love of God and then be willing to love others. We need to make our love a humble act, not a self-serving one. That is something far beyond puppy love—it is something transformative.

Weekly Humility Practice

Tell the people you love that you love them. Then do something small to show them.

Monthly Humility Practice

Engage in some act of service. Look into opportunities to serve in your local community. Give preference to the marginalized and underserved.

Yearly Humility Practice

Reflect on who you need to reconcile with—who have you made an enemy or an other? Spend some time praying about what reconciliation with this person (or group) might look like and take steps over the coming year to bring that reconciliation about.

5.
GIVING PRAISE

From the desire of being praised,
Deliver me, Jesus.
From the fear of suffering rebukes,
Deliver me, Jesus.
That others may be praised and I unnoticed,
Jesus, grant me the grace to desire it.

The day before our offices closed for Christmas break, I was setting an out-of-office responder on my email, thinking about the holiday ahead. My boss stopped in my office to wish me a merry Christmas and said something I will never forget. He said, "I just want you to know, you are one of my best team leaders. Thank you for all you do." It was so simple, but I felt fantastic. That little bit of praise propelled me through the rest of the day and well into my break.

The words of praise that have had the most impact on me have been spoken in private. I suspect this is true for you as well. Perhaps your manager tells you what a great job you did on a project or copies you on an email to the company president giving you credit for a big sale. These moments of praise can be as simple as a friend remarking that you've lost weight or your spouse expressing gratitude that the two of you are married. Moments of affirmation are necessary for a healthy human psyche. They provide a valuable outside opinion about our worth

71

from people that matter most. We want other people to like us, but we really want the people we like to affirm us.

Of course, our desire for praise isn't limited to receiving it from the people that are close to us. We aren't going to turn down a compliment from a coworker or a classmate. Praise feels good. But, like anything good, we can take it too far. We can let our desire to be praised get the best of us. For me, one of the more challenging sets of petitions in the Litany of Humility revolves around giving and receiving praise.

FROM THE DESIRE OF BEING PRAISED

I have to admit that I cringe when I pray, *"From the desire of being praised, deliver me, Jesus."* I know that true humility requires a movement from getting praise to giving praise, and that movement must begin with our recognition of the ways that our desire to be praised has become distorted and destructive—but that doesn't mean that I like it.

I can be driven by praise. After all, if I've worked hard at something, I want some affirmation about it. But if praise becomes the end goal, my projects and activities become less about personal fulfillment, growth in holiness, or even fulfilling my duties and obligations and more about the affirmation I might receive from others. I look over my shoulder as I work to see who will notice and pat me on the back to say, "Great job, man—you're crushing it." When I start to think that way, I stop doing things the way that I should and I start to do them in a way that I expect will bring me praise.

There are three habits that many of us slip into when we desire praise. We choose work that others will notice rather than work that we should do; we redirect glory to ourselves; and we avoid giving and receiving rebukes, even with those we care about.

CHOOSING WORK THAT GETS US NOTICED

Imagine that there are two parts of a project—one part is the necessary research, foundational to the success of the endeavor, and the other part is writing and presenting a report based on the research. You may have, as you just read that scenario, found yourself gravitating to one of those two areas based on your gifts and interests. Some people enjoy doing behind-the-scenes research, and other people like writing or presenting papers. Now imagine that the role you would choose won't be credited with the report. If you wanted to do the background research, you are told that you will not be cited in the final report as being an essential part of this project; the person presenting the report will have his name attached to it, not yours. If you wanted to do the writing, imagine that you are told that you will actually be ghostwriting because the person doing the research has a bigger name and needs to be the sole credit on the project. You will work hard and contribute a major part of the final product, but no one will ever know. You will watch as the other person receives praise (that is due, since they completed 50 percent of the project), but you won't receive anything. Not even the head of your company will know the part you played.

Perhaps a more likely scenario is that you work on a big project but after successful completion no one thanks you, even personally. People just move on. We would be rightly frustrated by our lack of credit in the research scenario and understandably demoralized by a failure to be thanked after a big project is completed. Giving praise is important in boosting the morale of those we work with and affirming those we love. We need to hear praise once in a while; we aren't emotionless robots.

But what happens if the next time you are asked to do a big report and you can choose to do research or writing, you don't go with your natural choice but instead select the option that will gain you recognition? What happens if the next time a big project comes along, you remember you weren't even thanked for the last project, so you either don't do this one as well or you don't do it at all?

Our desire for praise can lead to unhappiness, sometimes without our realizing what is happening. We've all had experiences where someone else was praised for something we helped with (or even did most of). We learned growing up that the star batters get all the attention at the end of a baseball game, whereas the outfielder that did his job through nine innings or more is often forgotten. We are likely to thank our pastor after a good sermon, but unlikely to thank the custodial staff that keeps our church clean. I used to manage the presentations that accompanied lyrics during worship at my church, and our staff joked about how when things went right nobody said anything, but if things went wrong everyone made sure to let us know. Some jobs are inherently behind the scenes and ignored.

When we experience those thankless moments—being the outfielder, the custodial worker, or the one doing the job that nobody notices until it goes wrong—we look at the people receiving the praise and think, "I want to do what they do." Our human need for affirmation becomes a desire, and we start to seek it, rather than embracing what we love or what our job requires us to do.

It is a slippery slope when we start doing things simply because they will earn us praise. It begins with taking on projects and roles that we may not like.

In college, I declared premedicine and athletic training as my double major. They were the two most rigorous fields of study at my college and promised a future with a large income. Other people admired me and praised my work ethic and career choices, which made me proud. Unfortunately, I hated that course of study. I did well, but I didn't enjoy any of it. I was succeeding at something I disliked, and I realized that if I continued down this path, I would spend much of my life doing something that everyone except me loved. I changed my major, but I know a lot of people whose story is different. They have chosen what will gain them the most praise rather than what they love. They do what will be recognized as success rather than what they really want to do.

DIRECTING THE GLORY
TO OURSELVES

My son and daughter are always looking for affirmation. As of this writing, they are four and two-and-a-half (my daughter is quick to point out the "half"). They want my wife and me to praise them, and at this age that is perfectly normal. They look over their shoulder to see if I am paying attention as they build train tracks, and they bring my wife pictures they color. We praise them for what they do, but we also teach them to praise each other. It is wonderful to see them encourage each other in their little projects. But at their age, they also compete. They each try to win more attention than the other and sometimes seek to steal praise.

Many, if not most, adults haven't completely grown up, including me. At work, I still look over my shoulder to see if my boss and coworkers are looking. If I were speaking out loud, I would be saying something like this: "Did you see that I completed that project way ahead of schedule? Have you heard from my team about how amazing our last meeting was? Don't you want to affirm me and tell me what a stellar job I am doing?" I become jealous of other people when I see them getting attention rather than me. I want to bump in front of them and say, "That thing you did looks great, but did you know that I also did this awesome thing?"

False humility manifests itself in a lot of ways. There are moments when we think that we are acting humbly, but we are actually just showing off. One of my favorite terms for this is "humblebrag." A humblebrag isn't easy to pull off, but once you've mastered the art, it can become a part of any conversation.

Essentially, you find a way to brag about something while still sounding humble about it. The goal of the humblebrag is to gain praise and affirmation from others without looking like you are trying to gain praise and affirmation.

Let's say you've been on a diet plan and have lost a lot of weight, but nobody has commented on it. You have an opportunity to pass on the macaroni and cheese, and you say, "Oh, no, thanks. That's loaded with carbs and fat. I'm on this new diet and it has been amazing—I've lost twenty pounds, but it isn't about the number, it's about my health."

See what happened there? An opportune moment to share about something you are proud of came up, and so you dropped the humblebrag. You gave the amount of weight you lost, then immediately walked it back to say it really isn't about the number. You are trying to look humble (like someone who doesn't care about appearance but about health) but also want other people to praise you for the hard work you've put in.

Unfortunately, opportune moments usually come up when someone else is receiving praise. We call this one-upping. You might know somebody who does that, or maybe you've been guilty of one-upping in a conversation as well. The humblebrag is one way to soften the edges of our desire to one-up another person. Thinking back to our experience with one-uppers, we realize how annoying they can be. It is irritating to be around someone who only wants to speak about himself and be in the spotlight.

The humblebrag isn't limited to in-person interactions. It's easy to post the #humblebrag on social media, which brings us back to the question of how authentic we are in what we post online. Do we curate our best, most praiseworthy moments for everyone to see in order to direct praise toward ourselves?

We need to honestly ask ourselves what our intentions are before we tap "post." Are we looking for praise, or are we authentically trying to share a bit of our lives? Are we seeking to inspire others by sharing our struggles and small victories with weight loss, or are we glossing over the tough details to make our successes appear effortless? Any intention that is derived from a desire to be praised is ultimately destructive. This isn't always easily discernible. It can be difficult to weed through the mess of our motivations, especially if we aren't used to parsing through what we actually think and feel. Recognizing the inclination to one-up or humblebrag and stopping it is critical to growth in humility and, in some cases, to sustaining and growing our relationships. If we aren't careful, we can easily move from the annoying friend that is always dropping the humblebrag to someone who is actually stealing praise from others in a kind of "praise plagiarism."

STEALING PRAISE

Every college student has heard the lecture about their school's plagiarism policy. Most universities have a low or zero tolerance. If you copy the work of another person without proper citation or outside of acceptable rules, you may automatically fail that assignment or course, or even be expelled. Since students are awarded grades and, ultimately, degrees based on their work, it makes sense that a university would severely penalize any person that steals the work of another and tries to pass it off as their own. Unfortunately, once we graduate we forget those lectures about stealing the intellectual work of another. We may not plagiarize something outright, but we may engage in praise plagiarism more often than we realize.

I've spent many years as an editor of curriculum resources, and one of the hardest conversations to have with a writer is about plagiarism. It doesn't happen often but is always awkward. The resources that I help publish do not have author names attached to them. A writing team creates them and gets compensated for the work. The team members aren't ghostwriters; even though no name is applied to the curriculum, they are all welcome to use us for references and letters of recommendation, and can use their work for us in portfolios. We always vouch for the authenticity of that work. Despite this, writers still hand in work, on occasion, that isn't their own.

I used to struggle to understand why, especially since the team members weren't receiving public credit for the work, but after one particular conversation with a writer I realized why some writers plagiarize. The reason wasn't to gain fame or recognition—they simply didn't want to give the appearance that they messed up an assignment or handed in poor work. It may have been that they came up against a tight deadline and wanted to turn something in on time. Maybe they felt uncomfortable with a given topic so they chose to copy and paste from a website, hoping that nobody would notice. Sometimes it was just an accident. For a writer, it isn't hard to catch. There are lots of programs that recognize copied work. For work outside of publishing, plagiarism takes a different form.

Praise theft is the plagiarism of the workplace and a toxin that can infect and destroy our relationships. Praise theft happens when someone accepts affirmation for something they didn't do, or they intentionally hop in at the end of a project or other activity in order to claim a share of the praise. In the most sinister cases, it is intentionally done, often by those in leadership positions. There is nothing more disheartening for an employee than to work hard on a project, only to have those higher on the organizational chart take all the credit for it. It is a self-seeking behavior and reveals a severe lack of confidence on the part of leaders in an organization. Insecure in their own positions, they fear that the accomplishments of those below them will somehow hinder their ability to maintain their job. So, when commended privately for a project by their boss, they don't share the glory. These situations can be maddening for an employee. A leader assures you that you will get the credit you deserve for a project, but you never hear from her.

One key virtue that great leaders exhibit is humility. A simple way that leaders demonstrate humility is in the way they

distribute praise. When Jim Collins, whom we met in the intro-
duction, asked leaders about the success of their companies, the
leaders often pointed to other departments or areas. They cited
specific people doing specific things, and chalked their leadership up to luck. Those leaders probably possess an incredible
amount of talent and are gifted with leadership, but humility
prevents them from taking that praise for themselves. These
kinds of leaders are trusted by those that follow them. They know
that the praise they give out is authentic.

Leaders that lack humility act in the opposite way. They are
quick to place blame on others for the shortcomings or failures of
the company, but are even faster in pointing to the ways in which
they made the company a success. These kinds of leaders create
a culture that is, well, all about them. In the short term, these
leaders receive public praise. They make shareholders happy and
probably make a lot of employees happy with bonuses, stock
sharing, and higher salaries . . . at least for a little while. Some
people are driven by money and don't care about praise as much,
but many of us want to know that what we are doing matters.
People who want their work to matter are the first to leave companies being driven by prideful leaders. Eventually those moti-
vated by money tire of being blamed for problems they didn't
create, as well. They leave. We can only handle so much praise
theft before we walk away.

Why do we do it? Why do we steal praise from others, even
plagiarizing work in the process? Why do we become one-uppers
or humblebraggers? For the same reason my kids (the same ones
that want praise) sometimes lie about what they did wrong.

FROM THE FEAR OF
SUFFERING REBUKES

The first time my son lied to me about something he did wrong
was hilarious. I had to try not to laugh out loud. That is one of

the hardest parts of parenting—not laughing when your kids do something funny but also wrong or dangerous. It sends a mixed message and usually ends with someone jumping off a couch into a pile of pillows while narrowly missing the end table because you laughed when they did it the first time. In this case, my son took a cookie off the table. I had put the cookies out to give to him and his sister after dinner, but he found them before that. There we were, standing in the kitchen, his hands and face covered in chocolate guilt as he told me that he didn't eat the cookie. He never broke eye contact and said it with a straight face, only stopping to flick his tongue out to lick some chocolate from the top of his lip. How do you not laugh out loud in that situation? We went back and forth before he finally confessed that he had eaten a cookie. He had no clue how I knew, though, because I was in the other room when he took it (again, hilarious).

Kids lie about doing something wrong because they like praise and don't like rebuke. Just like the rest of us. That's the second petition from the Litany of Humility we've got to reflect on when it comes to praise: *"From the fear of suffering rebukes, deliver me, Jesus."*

A rebuke is a sharp criticism or disapproval. Jesus uses the term in Luke 17:3: "If your brother sins, rebuke him." In this context, a rebuke isn't simply a criticism of our clothes or disapproval of our taste in music. If someone is authentically rebuking us, they are thinking of our salvation. In fact, a real rebuke can only be given by someone that has our best interest in mind and wants to see us grow. Perhaps that is why the second part of the above verse is, "and if he repents, forgive him." If a person offers us a rebuke, they aren't doing it out of malice. To the contrary, they are offering us something valuable to help us grow.

Most people don't give or receive rebukes in our current culture, for two reasons. First, we don't receive this kind of criticism well, so we are afraid to give it. Second, we keep our sins private and far from those we are close to out of fear they might see us as a bad person. Concealed sin can't be rebuked by those that can't see it.

PLAYING THE CRITIC

One area where I needed to grow as a writer was in receiving criticism. When you write, you pour your heart into your work; at least that is the romantic way of looking at it. You've also poured a lot of time, energy, frustration, excitement, and anxiety into that writing. When you send your work to someone to edit or review, there is a feeling of hopeful anticipation and crippling fear. The person reviewing your work might come back with, "Wow, this is the most amazing thing I've ever read! I am glad it was a digital copy, because any paper copy would have been ruined by the tears of joy I shed whilst reading it." Writers actually think this kind of stuff.

If the person serving as our editor doesn't care about us, the above is the kind of response they may offer. They might point out some minor grammatical mistakes but won't touch the content for fear of offending us. They know how hard we worked, and they don't want us to be disappointed. Meanwhile, anyone else who reads our work will remark about how poorly connected everything is, how the main themes get lost, and how they couldn't make it through a few paragraphs.

A good editor is a critical one. Good editors aren't critiquing our work simply because they enjoy the power of the red pen, but because they want it to be the very best reflection of who we are. In fact, editing may be one of the humblest professions that exists. Editors' names are rarely printed in the books they edit, and they are forced to deal with starry-eyed writers' fragile egos. (Note to my editor: Does this buy me any sympathy through my editing process?)

Much like a good editor, a good friend is willing to help us look critically at our lives and behavior. We don't help our friends by allowing them to persist in sin. We can rationalize our silence as respecting their decision or not wanting to judge, but we should call our silence what it actually is: selfish. We don't want to be uncomfortable in calling someone out when we know it will help them get better. There is this passage in the book of Proverbs that reads, "As iron sharpens iron, so one person sharpens another," (Proverbs 27:17 NIV). If our criticism helps someone to be sharper, that is a good thing. But if iron is sharpening iron, it means that in the process we are also growing and that can be uncomfortable.

Offering rebuke is not easy. We think of how we feel and how we don't like to hear criticism. There is a reason why we call it "suffering a rebuke," because sometimes it hurts. It isn't fun. "Wow, thanks for calling me out on this horrible thing I've been doing that has been hurting me, others, and even putting my salvation in jeopardy," is a statement no person has said when hearing a rebuke. They might say it eventually, but in the moment it is awful. We think about that awfulness anytime we have a moment to speak up or to stay silent. So, since we don't like it, we stay silent and hope that everyone else will return the kindness.

SUFFERING REBUKES WELL

The key to really embracing humility through giving praise lies in how we learn to suffer rebuke from others. The best way to learn to do that is to learn how to rebuke ourselves.

We need to make it a point to be inward seeking when things go wrong, and outward seeking when things go right. For many people, it is the opposite. When some company leaders see success, they are quick to attribute it to a new policy or initiative they enacted, but when something goes wrong, they look down the ladder to see where the error occurred (since it couldn't have possibly started at the top). They look at other managers, employees, or even seasonal stress to explain why something didn't work. These kinds of leaders can't handle criticism because they never criticize themselves. That mentality is inward seeking when it comes to praise, but outward seeking when it comes to blame.

We can adopt that same mentality in our relationships. When something is wrong, we look to blame someone or something else, but when things are good we believe that we are doing all the work. This type of relationship eventually becomes toxic if we never take ownership for our actions, can't accept criticism (because we never admit guilt or responsibility for mistakes), and, perhaps most critically, never offer praise.

If we really value personal development, we welcome rebuke, and we start by rebuking ourselves. Pastor Andy Stanley said in his *Leadership* podcast, "The common denominator in all my bad decisions is me." Even if we aren't fully culpable, we still play a role in the bad things that happen. Perhaps our role was small, but we still need to reflect on it first. I've rushed into battle over an issue too quickly many times—whether it was a problem at work or an issue in a relationship   and been embarrassed as I realized I was at fault.

If I had started with self-reflection, asking, "What did I do in this situation that is contributing to the problem or may be the problem itself?" I could have saved myself that embarrassment. When I am the first to call myself out, rebuke becomes easier to bear. More often than not, I've already determined what the issue of concern is and the rebuke gives me new perspective. The rebuke helps me grow. It isn't easy to hear, but since I am in the practice of rebuking myself, I understand the need.

Rebukes also help me filter levels of criticism. I listen to all criticism, but give it varying weight depending on the source and circumstances. Some people criticize me digitally. I get an email or a tweet, and for a moment I consider what they are say-ing—provided they've signed the comment with a real name (or sent it from a real account) and are courteous. If there is some truth that catches me, I think more about it. If the person is my direct supervisor or team leader, I give the rebuke much more weight. If it is a friend, I think even more deeply about it. If my wife offers a rebuke, I don't ever brush it off without considering it for at least the next few hours or days.

If we've already engaged in self-reflection, it is easier to listen to and accept rebukes from others. When instead we jump right in, arguing or trying to justify our behavior, two things tend to happen.

First, this sort of reaction hardens our hearts and reveals our pride. We are not-so-subtly saying to the person offering criticism, "What you think is wrong—I am perfect and above your critique or rebuke; I don't even need to listen." Second, people respond by making a point to avoid telling us hard truths in the future that could help us grow. This is a challenge that many people in management face, especially if they struggle to receive criticism from peers or those whom they supervise. It is already difficult to offer honest feedback to your boss, but it becomes exponentially so when you have witnessed your supervisor react poorly to critical feedback in the past. In those situations, employees hesitate to offer constructive comments and instead give empty praise.

Since we desire praise (even if it is empty), we accept poison pills of praise. Management may *hear* all the positive comments they want to hear from colleagues while things are actually falling apart beneath them. Eventually, the poison pills of praise hit our bloodstream. Leaders that can't receive criticism lose control of their company. They exist in an echo chamber as their organization crumbles around them. Jesus even cautions against this: "Woe to you when all speak well of you, for their ancestors treated the false prophets in this way" (Lk 6:26). If all we ever hear is praise with no signs of conflict, we should get cautious— we may also be living in an echo chamber.

The same thing can happen in marriages or friendships. When a spouse responds poorly to rebuke or criticism, the loved one may stop offering it. For a while they offer empty praise, but eventually that stops, too. What is the point of praising someone you love if you can't point out and talk about the things that are problems? Empty praise fades into silence, and then the relationship falls apart.

By accepting rebuke and considering carefully the criticisms we receive, we grow in humility. That criticism must start with ourselves. When we become open to the criticism of ourselves and others, we can start sharing praise.

THAT OTHERS MAY BE PRAISED AND I UNNOTICED

The most challenging petition of this section of the Litany of Humility is undoubtedly this one: *"That others may be praised and I unnoticed, Jesus, grant me the grace to desire it."*

It is one thing for other people to be praised, but going unnoticed is tough. This is why learning to embrace rebuke and to be able to rebuke yourself is key. It gives us a disposition toward a humble heart that is able to thrive off criticism as much as praise. And when we can grow from both criticism and praise, we become much more comfortable praising other people.

We can take inspiration for praising others from St. Paul and his letter to the Philippians: "Do nothing out of selfishness or out of vainglory; rather, humbly regard others as more important than yourselves, each looking out not for his own interests, but also everyone for those of others" (2:3–4). This bit of wisdom sums up where we are going in this section of the Litany of Humility. If we regard others' interests and needs rather than our own prideful desires, we won't miss opportunities to praise them.

If we pray that others will be praised and we will be unnoticed, we must also start living that desire. Thankfully, there is plenty we can do to cooperate with the grace that Christ will give us to live these petitions. It begins with giving something away.

GIVING IT ALL AWAY

During his travels, Jesus met a man looking for praise. In Mark's gospel, this guy is simply called "the rich man." He approaches Jesus and asks what he must do to get to heaven. The rich man is setting up for an epic humblebrag; he knows Jesus is a respected teacher and that his words hold a great deal of weight. Jesus sees through the act but plays along. He responds, "You know the commandments: 'You shall not kill; you shall not commit adultery; you shall not steal; you shall not bear false witness; you shall not defraud; honor your father and your mother'" (Mk 10:19).

Now it is time for the rich man to drop his humblebrag: "Teacher, all of these I have observed from my youth" (Mk 10:20). The rich man is seemingly also a righteous man. But Jesus isn't finished. "Jesus, looking at him, loved him and said to him, 'You are lacking in one thing. Go, sell what you have, and give to [the] poor and you will have treasure in heaven; then come, follow me'" (v. 21).

The man goes away sad, "for he had many possessions" (v. 22).

The rich man desires praise from Jesus, but instead is rebuked. It turns out that the rich man wasn't observing the law as completely as he thought, and Jesus lovingly calls him out on it. Jesus invites him to let go of his wealth so he can follow Jesus.

This is more than just giving stuff away; this is giving up status. The rich man's wealth allows him to be somebody. In the Gospel of Luke, this same character is referred to as a "rich official," meaning he holds some kind of public office. He is known and recognized. To leave that behind and follow Jesus means becoming a nobody. It means going unnoticed.

When it comes to giving praise, we are called to be overly generous. We are called to give what we have. We may not have money to give away, but we do have the power of our words and affirmation. We may worry that in giving this away freely, we will have nothing left—that other people will be noticed but we won't be.

But we need to confront that lie. Did you see what Jesus asked this man? He asked him to become a disciple; that is bigger than riches and notoriety. Jesus invites us to do the same. Giving praise generously may not seem natural to you, so here are five practical steps to make it second nature.

1. Start Close. Become intentional about the praise and affirmation you give to those closest to you. Oftentimes it is our friends, family, and spouse who hear praise from us the least. Although these relationships are bound by a deeper level of intimacy (and in the case of marriage, sacramental grace), they are also the easiest to neglect. Find ways to authentically praise those you love. Challenge yourself to find something small to praise them for. It is easy to praise others for big moments and accomplishments (and we should), but if we become intentional about also noticing the little things, then we take our praise to a new level.

2. Know the Limits, but Don't Hold Back. When it comes to praise, there is such a thing as too much—and praise becomes too much when it is inauthentic. I remember getting a participation trophy the year my team lost the championship baseball game. That kind of affirmation wasn't necessary and, in some ways, was detrimental. We don't need to excessively praise small accomplishments; sometimes that draws away from the value of big achievements and can make our sincerity questionable.

However, if someone does something you are really excited about, don't hold back your enthusiasm. If you think a friend has really grown in her profession or talent, let that show in your praise. I once had a friend tell me that he wasn't going to affirm someone who had really grown professionally because he wanted her "to stay humble." I was taken aback by the statement. It really isn't up to us to worry about whether our praise will give someone a big head, except perhaps in the case of our own children. But if we are having that conversation with ourselves and using it to determine whether or not to praise a coworker or friend for something they did well, we need to check our own pride. We aren't the judge and jury of someone's humility. We can challenge them if necessary, but withholding praise when it is due because we don't want someone to get too prideful is a bit over the top.

3. Send Positivity Downward. If you are a leader, parent, teacher, or someone else with some authority and direction over others, make sure you are continually sending positivity downward to those that you serve in your leadership role. Sometimes people worry that offering too much praise can cause someone's work ethic to dwindle. This is why private praise is actually critical in an organization. For many, the individual conversation in which a supervisor, teacher, or coach offers you praise is much more meaningful than a public affirmation, especially if you trust your leader to be genuine. That kind of private praise is motivating, not sloth inducing.

As a leader in any capacity, we can't allow ourselves to fall into the trap of only giving praise on rare occasions. I know a few people in leadership roles who believe withholding frequent praise makes it matter more when they offer it. I can promise that your family, students, and employees do not agree. Make it a point to offer praise often, but again, don't just offer empty praise. Find real things to affirm and use those for a springboard to praise.

4. Take a Background Role. When we ask that others would be praised and we go unnoticed we need to also practice being unnoticed. Find things you can do that are background roles that nobody will notice you doing. This could be something you do at work, for your friends, or with your family. The goal of the task is to complete something of value (though it may still be menial) and do it without anyone noticing. In this way you can put in work but forgo the praise.

There is a particular task that I do at my office. A while ago I decided that when I saw this particular task needed to be done, I would do it. I don't call attention to it, I don't make a big deal out of it, and I don't ask others to help do it. I do it because it needs to get done, but it is also a spiritual practice. I need to work on being unnoticed and that job helps me do it.

5. Give Praise Where it is Due. The final step in giving praise is to make sure we are offering praise back to God. This is different than offering thanksgiving to God for the good things we are blessed with. Praising God is prayer to God just because God is God. We need to offer praise to God because it balances our relationship. It refocuses us on the reality that we are not God and this breeds humility. Through that humility, we become comfortable with being unnoticed when we do work because we recognize that God sees us, and that is pleasing.

Become a person that offers generous praise and embraces the moments you are unnoticed, criticized, or rebuked. The praise that others offer won't dry up; but you will appreciate it more while placing less of an emphasis on how it drives you. You will be liberated from the tension between doing work that matters and doing work that gets you noticed and will become a better leader, teammate, friend, and partner.

Weekly Humility Practice

Find one thing to praise a friend, spouse, or coworker for every week that doesn't involve you or result in a humblebrag from you.

Monthly Humility Practice

Take up a task that needs to be done, and that you can do quietly. Don't let anyone know that you do it.

Yearly Humility Practice

Review people in your life that have grown, achieved substantial accomplishments, or are approaching milestones in their lives. Create a calendar of upcoming events and commit to writing cards to send over the course of the year, offering genuine praise and affirmation to each of these people.

6.
EMPOWERING
THOSE AROUND ME

From the desire of being extolled,
Deliver me, Jesus.
From the fear of being forgotten,
Deliver me, Jesus.
That others may be preferred to me
in everything,
Jesus, grant me the grace to desire it.

I sat backstage alone in a room that was too big for just one person. I could hear the crowd of people, numbered in the tens of thousands, in the arena. I shifted in my chair and looked over the notes for my talk even though I knew the outline perfectly. I had spent months anticipating this moment, realizing it would be too much to comprehend.

I was about to speak at the biggest English-language event at World Youth Day in Krakow, Poland, and I knew that I didn't belong there.

The event was a night of praise, a message, and eucharistic adoration—called a "Night of Mercy"—and I was part of the ministry team for that evening. The other team members were two well-known and well-traveled musicians. They were easily recognizable to almost anyone showing up that night. The bishop leading eucharistic adoration and also preaching was extremely popular around the world—he had been on television shows and the radio, and had written some incredible things. If possible, he was even more well-known than the musicians.

Then there was me—with a name that precious few people knew. A random guy on a bill of talent that heavily outweighed anything I had ever done. I found out I was giving the message for the night—a twenty-minute talk—several weeks before the event. I was excited but also terrified. I felt like I didn't fit in with the rest of the team. In the weeks leading up to World Youth Day, my fears were echoed in snide comments people made about how I was the weak link and how "there has to be somebody on the team that is the worst person—guess that's you." By the time I arrived, I truly believed I was in the wrong spot.

Those fears caused a counteremotion of pride to rise up in me. Like a scorned sports player, I developed a chip on my shoulder. I would make them know my name. I would make sure that, after that night, the world knew who I was. They wouldn't think I was the weakest link anymore.

In prayer and after sharing these things with my wife, I realized how stupidly prideful I was acting. I needed to keep myself in check—I needed to desire success for the right reason, namely to proclaim the Gospel well, rather than to find some kind of vindication for being chosen. So I wrote a prayer in my journal asking God to keep me humble. The first line was blunt: "At the end of today, may my name be forgotten." The rest of the prayer followed the same tone.

I prayed it before I walked onto the stage alongside the band. I prayed it, but I didn't really mean it. I prayed it because I knew that was the humble thing to do, but my heart still wanted public affirmation. I wanted the big win. I wanted my name to be remembered after that night.

I've learned that God answers half-hearted prayers if he knows they are what we really need. So I gave my talk, and it went well. My friends and coworkers complimented me. I spoke to roughly 25,000 people in the arena, outside of the arena, and all through the world on a live broadcast. The venue was sold out, filled with English-speaking pilgrims from all over the world. The night was incredible. People wrote news articles about it. I will never forget reading the first one, excited to see what they would say about my amazing talk. But they didn't say anything. In fact, my name wasn't even mentioned. The same was true for the next article I read, and the one after that. In the days that followed, most of the major news articles in the Catholic world either omitted my name or listed it as a sort of footnote to the glory of that evening. It was like I was never there at all—the weak link of the night that was totally forgotten after it was all over.

I don't know how your relationship with God is, or if God has ever revealed his presence to you or given you a sign of his love. My signs come in the form of answered prayers that I don't want answered. They come in the realization that God knows me better than I know myself, and knows that even my half-hearted prayers are faith enough for him to do some big things in my life. I needed the humility that came with my name being forgotten, and I also needed the consolation of knowing that if God granted me that prayer, it meant that God wanted to use the experience to help me become holier.

WINNING BIG

I once took a work personality test with the team that I lead. The test showed us very useful information about our individual work habits and our manner of interacting as a team. I was shocked at how accurate my results were; they described me perfectly. One particular line stood out in my assessment: "Doesn't just want to win; wants to win with flair and high recognition."

I remember trying not to smile when I read that line. I was both embarrassed and proud at how true the statement rang. I didn't just want to succeed; I wanted to succeed at such a high level that people could not help but notice and pour out praise. I wanted to prove people wrong—prove them so wrong that they apologized for how wrong they were via email or (if I was lucky) a handwritten note with a Starbucks gift card in it. That desire got me in a lot of trouble, especially when working with a team. I started to make things mostly about me and my recognition, my name, and my win.

It didn't just get me in trouble as a manager, but in my relationships. That desire to win and be recognized took over all areas of my life. It turned me into a workaholic. I constantly checked my email, obsessively checked in on projects, worked long hours, and if a member of my team dropped the ball, I made sure that they heard about it. After all, we weren't just trying to win—we were trying to win big!

FROM THE DESIRE OF BEING EXTOLLED

What the work assessment told me was that I enjoy being extolled. That's a phrase contained in one of the petitions of the Litany of Humility: "*From the desire of being extolled, deliver me, Jesus.*"

There is a difference between being extolled and being praised. Being praised is personal and private, whereas being extolled is public and exuberant. It isn't just one person complimenting you; it is an arena of people shouting your praises and chanting your name.

It is the kind of gushing, over-the-top public praise that makes us both embarrassed and proud.

Desiring this praise can make us miserable to be around. It is one thing to work for the praise of others and to fear rebukes, but when we give in to that desire for massive public praise, we can turn into self-absorbed monsters.

IT'S MY STAGE

If you've ever been affirmed by your boss during a staff meeting or had an article written about one of your accomplishments, you know the feeling of owning the spotlight. Being extolled can seemingly promise us job security, recognition, fame, money, and respect. But any celebrity knows how fleeting public praise can be—one day you are popular and in the news, and the next day you are forgotten. If we aren't careful, receiving public praise can quickly lead to wanting more and fearing the loss of it.

So we work harder. We keep for ourselves the big projects that will win us affirmation. We put work and our desire for recognition first. We strive to be noticed. We become difficult to work with because we make every project about ourselves. In staff meetings we try to grab the spotlight.

That is where the desire starts to isolate us. We don't like to share the glory. We believe that, if we share even part of it, there will be less for us. Do you know a leader or have a friend who thinks this way? Maybe you are reading this and thinking, "Actually, that person is me."

FROM THE FEAR
OF BEING FORGOTTEN

Our desire to be extolled largely stems from a fear that we will be forgotten. Being forgotten, left out, or becoming obsolete is worse than being gossiped about. The adage "Any publicity is good publicity" affirms that even negative public comments are better than no one talking about us at all. To be unseen or forgotten? That is awful.

I was the wrestling team captain my senior year of high school. It was a big accomplishment for me and something I was very proud of. In elementary school, I was not athletic and was bullied a lot for that reason. Even through junior high school I hardly considered myself an athlete, so to be captain of a varsity team in high school was a big deal. Unfortunately, I was injured midway through the season. A couple years later, I visited the school and happened to look in the logbook of all the team captains for varsity sports. Proudly, I went to look up my name and relive my moment of glory, but it wasn't there. Whether it was intentionally left off because I didn't finish the season or it was an error—my name was gone. It was as though I was never on the team that year at all. Maybe it was a minor thing to be upset about, but I was upset. I was forgotten.

The fear of being forgotten can drive us to do some wild things. We will take on extra projects at work because we don't want our supervisors to think we are slacking and pass us over for a promotion. If we feel like we are being neglected in a friendship or romantic relationship, we may start to act irrationally, becoming overly sensitive or even smothering to make sure we are remembered and cared for. Even kids demonstrate this behavior if they feel like their parents are ignoring them—they act out, break a toy, or throw a tantrum in order to be remembered. The Litany of Humility anticipates this fear as we petition for grace, saying, *"From the fear of being forgotten, deliver me, Jesus."*

Both our fear of being forgotten and our desire to be extolled play off some of our biggest anxieties, especially when it comes to work and personal recognition. We reason that, if we want to be successful and get ahead in our company and in the world of business networking, we need to find ways to win and win big. We need to get the sort of recognition and admiration that warrants people extolling us on various platforms. We set up a false dichotomy that says if we aren't being extolled or spending time in the spotlight, then we are fading into the land of forgotten people. We don't want that, so we push harder to be recognized but are never comfortable. We may take on more and more responsibilities in an effort to prove our worth, but eventually we will burn out.

THAT OTHERS MAY BE
PREFERRED TO ME IN . . .
EVERYTHING?

A remedy exists within the Litany of Humility, but it is difficult to pray: *"That others may be preferred to me in everything, Jesus, grant me the grace to desire it."*

We worry that if we pray this petition earnestly and work toward it, it might mean that in some instances we are forgotten. The reality is that we aren't forgotten—we just become a footnote.

Helping people become preferred to you may seem like an awkward concept at first, but there is a better name for it, especially as it relates to a work environment. We call it "empowerment." The word appears in a variety of contexts, but here we understand it as enabling someone to do a task with a higher degree of success than they could do on their own. The kicker is that when we empower people, we step back and allow them to receive the glory.

Real empowerment is setting someone up for success but letting them also enjoy the fruits. Real empowerment in the corporate world is scary, so people often settle for "empowerment light," which amounts to supported delegation. When we replace empowerment with supported delegation, it looks similar to this: A manager has a task that she realizes she does not have time for, but also doesn't want to be left out of. She asks an employee to work on the project, saying things like, "I want to empower you to take this on." At various points, though, she interjects and starts to micromanage the project, even taking over at different points along the way. When the project is revealed, she steps forward to claim credit. The desire to be extolled and the fear of being forgotten both come full throttle, and there is no sharing of the spotlight in the final moment when it matters.

That is supported delegation, and it is demoralizing. It makes any promise of empowerment or ownership of a work project meaningless.

Empowering others means that we work so that they actually become the preferred authority in a given area. Real empowerment enables someone else to operate and make decisions independent of your authority; in fact, you empower them with your authority. They act on your behalf, and you trust them. This is liberating in a work situation for not only the employee but the employer; it frees up those in leadership positions to do more. It is also critical in family life. Parents should empower their children to do chores, clean up, and make important decisions. The challenge is that when we empower others, we also let go of the praise that comes with doing the work ourselves.

As a leader, when you empower others to complete a task, you need to allow them to enjoy the fruits of their success without stepping in to say, "Well, you know, if it weren't for me that project would never have gotten completed." As a parent, if you empower your daughter to succeed on a big project, you need to allow her to enjoy the spotlight rather than stepping in to say, "You know, I taught her that." Empowerment means allowing someone to own what they are doing, and it requires an act of humility and confronting the fear that we will be forgotten.

As parents, we often worry that if we empower our kids too much they won't need us anymore. Some parents worry so much about their children failing that they hold them in an extended period of childhood. They don't empower their kids to get jobs, earn money, or go on dates. The result is that many young people enter college and the workforce without employment experience or well-developed social skills.

If as leaders we never empower those we lead, we wind up shouldering more and more of the burden of our organization's work, and those below us never improve. If we fear that by empowering others we might lose our foothold and be forgotten, we simply start a burnout clock that ticks away every moment we are at work. We have to let that fear go and recognize that empowerment of others doesn't result in our being forgotten—it results in us becoming a footnote.

Footnotes aren't bad things. They give us a fuller version of the story, but if we are being honest, most people aren't looking at the footnotes. But the author put the footnotes there for a reason—either to convey more information or to cite a source. Good authors don't plagiarize; they want their readers to know where their work came from. That is empowerment. We give people what they need to be successful, and they remember us. Is it worth being a footnote to a great success story? Would you be satisfied empowering someone to do something great if it meant you were seemingly forgotten? There is a boy with bread that knows the answer.

GIVING UP DINNER

If you are familiar with the New Testament, you know that the Gospels of Matthew, Mark, and Luke contain a lot of similar material. Scholars refer to these three books as the synoptic gospels because they share so much. Then there is the Gospel of John. The structure of John's gospel is different, and it contains material that does not appear in the synoptics. Some scholars have speculated that, since this was the last gospel written, John wrote it at the urging of both Peter and Mary, who asked that some important details be included from the life of Jesus that were omitted from the synoptic gospels. These include incidents that only Mary and Peter would know about, such as the wedding at Cana and the final conversations between Peter and Jesus.

Some important events are described in all four gospels. The story of Jesus's death and resurrection is one such narrative. Another is the feeding of the five thousand, which recalls the multiplication of a few loaves of bread and some fish into a quantity that feeds well over five thousand people. This story appears in the Gospels of Matthew, Mark, and Luke, but John adds one detail the prior three missed. He includes where the loaves and fish came from.

In all four accounts, there is a problem. Many people are hungry but have nowhere to get food. The question is asked where they might find food for the crowd. In John 6:9, Andrew (the brother of Peter) responds to the question: "There is a boy here who has five barley loaves and two fish." That small detail is left out of the other three accounts of the same miracle story. If you are familiar with the story, you know that everyone receives more than enough to eat. It is a major miracle in the ministry of Jesus.

I've always found that one detail interesting. Perhaps the scholars are correct and Peter helped John with his gospel, making him privy to this small detail. Really, it amounts to a footnote. The boy isn't important to the story—but to the disciple Andrew (and perhaps also Peter), the detail was worth remembering, enough for John to include it. Without that boy, the miracle won't happen.

Can you imagine the boy's position, though? He is probably heading home from the market with food for his family when he gets caught up in this crowd. He has food and he has a choice—he can lend what he has, or he can keep it for himself. Nobody would have blamed him if he said, "Look, my family spent money for this food. We need it. I can't give it to you, because I am worried about what might happen to them."

When it comes to empowering others, we can have a similar thought process: "I can't empower other people; I'm not sure what they will do with that empowerment. Plus, it means letting go of things I hold on to—what if I don't get them back? What if it costs me my job? What if I have to clean up the mess?" The temptation is to hold tightly to what we perceive as ours, and nobody really blames us when we do. The world is a competitive place.

But the boy in the Gospel of John does give up the food, and something amazing happens. The miracle of the multiplication of the loaves and fish is a critical moment in Jesus' ministry. And it doesn't happen without that boy, who isn't even mentioned in three of the four gospels.

Would you be willing to be a footnote in the life of another person? The boy in the story likely left with more food than he came with, given how much was left over after all were fed. He received more than he brought, but we never find out any more about him. He gets one verse of credit, and not even a named credit. Just a boy with a basket. But he was at the center of it all. He got to see it happen. When we empower others, we bring them what we have so they can do something great. Sometimes that means being a footnote, but humility rejoices in being the footnote. It celebrates being forgotten if it means someone else is praised. We can only really embrace that attitude if we are confident and authentic. We can only accept the moments we are seemingly forgotten if we trust that God never forgets us.

And that is what I realized in the days after that World Youth Day. Incredible things happened that night—miraculous things. The presiding bishop said it was a defining moment of his priesthood. I watched an arena of 25,000 people fall totally silent in praise and adoration of Jesus Christ. I was a footnote to the glory of God.

You may be a footnote to the success story of someone else or to the moment a person's life changed completely. You may end up being a stepping stone to greater faith for another. You might help a coworker get a promotion, or you might empower a friend to finally start that business that really takes off. You will fear being forgotten, but you need to trust that what you receive in return is much better, even if nobody sees.

Weekly Humility Practice

Write your own prayer asking that you might be forgotten in the work you do, but that the name of Christ will be remembered through your actions. Make it a point to offer this prayer daily.

Monthly Humility Practice

Review your workload, and ask if there are any areas where you can empower someone else to become an expert.

Yearly Humility Practice

Determine what areas of responsibility you need to let go of, and allow someone else to become the preferred authority. Make the appropriate changes to allow this to happen.

7.
BECOMING
THE MENTOR

From the desire of being consulted,
Deliver me, Jesus.
From the fear of being suspected,
Deliver me, Jesus.
That others may be chosen and I set aside,
Jesus, grant me the grace to desire it.

"It doesn't say in my contract I have to get Aaron ready to play."
Brett Favre, a Hall of Fame quarterback in the NFL, spoke those
words about the new quarterback his team, the Green Bay Packers, had just drafted. Favre was a legend and had a storied career
in Green Bay, but when the team drafted a younger quarterback
as Favre neared retirement age, the writing was on the wall.

Favre's reaction to the draft pick was less than favorable. He
didn't like the new quarterback, and their relationship from the
first day was strained. He made it clear that he wasn't going to
teach Aaron Rodgers how to play in the NFL.

The draft of a new quarterback was the first in many frac-
tures in Favre's relationship with the Packers. After a couple of
dramatic seasons, Favre retired from football, but then came out
of retirement only months later and signed with a new team,
then was traded to one of the Packers' rivals. His behavior at
the end of his career and his refusal to gracefully transition the

leadership of his football team will unfortunately be among the things Favre is most remembered for.

He held a position of great influence and special privilege. He didn't want to give up that status, let alone transfer it to someone new. Aaron Rodgers was more than an adequate replacement for Favre, and now has his own storied career. It's an iconic sports story, but it happens everywhere.

I'M NOT GOING ANYWHERE

Organizations are filled with people entrenched in positions of leadership. Any of us can fall into this trap, whether it is as a volunteer or as an executive at a major company. We hang on tightly to our place in the center-stage spotlight, fearful that someone will replace us.

I knew a woman who held an elite position in her company. When she left the job, she hoped the company's management would feel the sting of her absence and call her to consult on new projects. But they didn't. They moved on.

Many of us have had this same thought when leaving an organization, especially if we aren't leaving on good terms. We think, "They will regret this. I am the only one who knows how to do my job." Some of this stems from the fear we discussed in the last chapter. We worry that we will be forgotten. Other times it comes from a fear of the unknown—if somebody else takes my job, what will I do? Who will I *be*?

When confronted with these situations, we can begin the process of becoming a mentor to another person, or we can make ourselves critical to the operation of our organization. The first route brings humility, while the second is perhaps one of the most insidious forms of pride.

FROM THE DESIRE
OF BEING CONSULTED

The petition from the Litany of Humility that executives, team leaders, and managers find most difficult is, *"From the desire of being consulted, deliver me, Jesus."* If you are in a management position, you want to be consulted on the decisions the people on your team make. There is a special kind of anxiety that comes along with finding out a team has made critical decisions on a project that you as leader knew nothing about until it was too late. The desire to be consulted is a desire to be an integral part of decision-making, even if it isn't necessary. There is a pride in being so important that people come to you to make decisions—even decisions that don't specifically relate to your area. We like being important and needed. It sends a simple message that feeds our ego: You are smart. You have a great skill set that other people don't have. We need you.

I worked with an intern who told me that he wanted to become a consultant to churches when he graduated from college. The idea revealed what he thought about his knowledge—despite being only twenty-two and possessing no experience of church life outside of volunteer work, he wanted to immediately have the respect that being a consultant would command. Consultants know something we don't. They have a specialized knowledge that we pay them to impart to us common folk. Why wouldn't he want to be a consultant? But he lacked the skills to play that role, at least right out of college. We had an honest conversation, and he changed course.

Rather than criticize the young intern, we need to empathize with him, because we all live out this disordered desire in some way. We say things like, "Well, if they would just ask me—I could tell them how to run this company!" We express our opinions—often unsolicited—via social media and over dinners. We jump in with our expertise, hoping someone will ask us to explain more. We long for people to sit at our feet, soaking up our knowledge.

Being consulted at work gives us a share and gives us control. Being consulted by our friends gives us a sense of superiority and makes us feel respected. Can you imagine how flattered you would be if tomorrow you walked into work and your boss said, "Hey, we've got a new project we are working on and we need your insight."

You would walk into that meeting with your head held high, proud that you were thought enough of to be asked to partici- pate. Until a sinking feeling of doubt crept in as you wondered to yourself, "What if I say the wrong thing . . . do I even belong here?"

THE GREAT IMPOSTER

"You have imposter syndrome."

I looked at my wife and tried to process the odd statement that had just issued forth from her mouth. "What?" I responded, unsure of what it was she was talking about.

"Imposter syndrome. I was reading about it today. You have it." I've always appreciated my wife's direct approach when speak- ing truth to me. I was still confused about what this affliction was that I didn't realize I had, so I asked her to explain.

She told me that imposter syndrome is when a person who has the skills, talent, and support to be in a position feels like they don't belong there. They get anxious about it and worry that at any moment other people will discover they are an imposter and blow their cover. As I listened, I realized that she was right.

I went through a competitive interview process for my job. I worked hard and proved myself over and over again, earning the support of my peers and my direct supervisors. I received consistently good annual reviews. Yet, despite all of this, some- times I believed I didn't belong. I felt like I had somehow fallen into this position and was barely coasting along, putting on a good show that couldn't last forever. "When they find out," I thought, "it's going to be awful and embarrassing." I imagined being in a staff meeting when somebody finally stood up and said, "Joel doesn't belong here! He is a fraud!" I also imagined this happening exclusively with an old English accent—it just feels more dramatic that way.

Imposter syndrome is a psychological maladaptation that causes us to believe we don't belong but somehow stumbled our way into wherever we are in life. This outlook can be quite destructive. If a husband has imposter syndrome in a marriage, he becomes overly protective and restrictive of his wife. Since he feels he somehow doesn't deserve to be married to her, he views any outside individual as a threat who might cause his wife to find out about the imposter. That situation can become really toxic, really fast.

In a work environment, a similar thing can happen. A person feels like she is underqualified (for a job that she is likely well qualified for) and that she somehow doesn't belong. The response is to overcompensate. If she can make herself indispensable in certain areas, then she has to be consulted and can prove her worth. Other employees, new hires, and even management become a threat because the individual worries that any of these people could blow her cover.

Not everyone experiences imposter syndrome. For me, it was something I needed to recognize and work through with the help of others. But we all experience a bit of the fear that comes with the new hire that might eventually replace us or the organizational realignment that threatens to shift our role. If we are in a romantic relationship, we may feel a twinge of jealousy when our significant other spends time with friends away from us and we wonder, "Will she have more fun with them than with me?"

FROM THE FEAR
OF BEING SUSPECTED

There is a particular fear that often accompanies the desire of being consulted—the fear of being suspected. We can pray for deliverance from this complementary fear with the simple petition "*From the fear of being suspected, deliver me, Jesus.*"

When we hear the word "suspected," we probably think in legal terms. We imagine *Law & Order* and think that this fear has to do with being suspected of committing a crime.

But being suspected in this context isn't about wrongdoing; it is about being credible. It is when other people, rather than wanting to consult you, question whether you actually have the ability and expertise to do your job or be brought into a conversation. We might say, "His expertise on the subject is suspect." If people start to question our abilities, opinions, and skills, it could have serious ripple effects in our lives.

Our response to the fear of being suspected is to entrench ourselves in our positions at work. We hoard knowledge and don't let other people into our process. We make ourselves seemingly irreplaceable. We stop listening to advice or feedback about how to do our work better, even if it would make our lives easier. This sort of job entrenchment is destructive because, while we may extend our career, we only delay the inevitable. Eventually, those around us realize that we are actually holding work back, rather than helping to get it done.

Our desire to be consulted can put us in the way of things that need to get done, and our fear of being suspected can cause us to become more deeply entrenched. Both are marks of pride. The response in humility is to become a mentor, someone that willingly shares knowledge and expertise.

A LOST ART

Sadly, mentorship is a lost art in much of our contemporary world. When we think about our own formation, we may recall one or two people that really invested in us, walked with us, and empowered us as mentors. Empowerment, as we have seen, is helping people grow in specific tasks and areas so they can be successful. Mentorship involves empowerment but is further reaching. It is an investment in the life of another person. Empowerment helps someone perform a task they aren't currently doing but that they can achieve with your help. It may be a specific task that you currently do. Mentorship trains someone to take your place completely. In the trade work world, mentorship is built into the fabric of learning a trade through apprenticeships. Elsewhere it is far less common. Mentorship involves a lot of work and time; it is a commitment to someone for a longer period of time than it takes to simply teach and empower them for a single task.

In a highly individualized culture like ours, it is no wonder mentorship is being overlooked. People are more concerned about their career aspirations, financial success, and job stability than they are with passing their knowledge on to others. More and more young people are growing up without knowing how to be an adult. While this stems from multiple causes, one large contributor is that many adults no longer take the time to mentor young people. We teach them, but we don't invest in them. We don't take them under our wing to help them learn to be an adult. We expect Google to help them figure all of that out. We reason that we simply don't have the time.

Mentorship requires a real person, not a book or a website. A mentor guides us and works alongside us as we learn, fail, and celebrate our accomplishments. Mentoring makes sense because we can't do our job forever. It prepares someone to take our place and, at best, do our job better than we did.

THAT OTHERS MAY BE
CHOSEN AND I SET ASIDE

Mentorship requires a humble perspective. We need to have the humility to say, "I do my job well, but if I help train someone to get past all the mistakes I made initially, then that person can become even better than I was and do my job someday better than I ever could." Mentorship doesn't make us obsolete; it gives us a spot in a workplace lineage. It doesn't diminish our worth in an organization, but rather increases it.

Recognizing the value of mentoring can help reduce the fear that inevitably arises when we think about becoming a mentor—what happens when the person I am mentoring surpasses me? In his book *Reinvent Yourself*, James Altucher wrote that oftentimes mentoring relationships end on bad terms because those being mentored surpass the mentor. Lacking humility is a fatal flaw for a mentor. Those who see their mentorship not as passing the torch, but as gaining a lifelong apprentice, experience wounded pride when their Robin takes over the Batman role. Eventually every apprentice ought to surpass a good mentor, and the best mentors are happy when it happens. They might even consider it the greatest measure of success. Praying the Litany of Humility is helpful in this regard—in particular the petition *"That others may be chosen and I set aside, Jesus, grant me the grace to desire it."*

This petition is straightforward. We ask God to give us the grace to want others to be chosen for tasks for which we might also be chosen. That presupposes that we are qualified for the same task. I'm not skilled at visual arts, so it isn't difficult to pray, "That others may be chosen as lead graphic designer and I set aside." But it is difficult for me to pray, "That other writers would be chosen for a big book project and I set aside." I need grace to pray that. As with any petition, we pray for the grace, but we also need to act upon it. That comes through mentorship.

TIMOTHY AND PAUL

Throughout the Bible there are numerous stories of mentorship. Naomi and Ruth, Moses and Joshua, Jesus and the disciples. One of the more developed narratives of mentorship involves Paul and Timothy. Paul mentions Timothy frequently in his letters, which gives us some insights into their relationship, but Luke also details their journeys in the Acts of the Apostles, and letters that Paul wrote specifically to Timothy are also preserved within the New Testament. These sources provide us with a spiritual template for mentorship—whether it is spiritual or professional. There are seven phases to Paul's mentorship of Timothy, and any mentoring relationship should follow these same seven phases, all with the goal of another being chosen as we are set aside.

1. Invite the Follower. Paul meets Timothy when he is passing through Lycaonia (see Acts 16:1-5). Timothy is already a disciple of Jesus but has not met Paul. Timothy's reputation precedes him, and Paul is informed that Timothy is an honorable man. When Paul finds out that Timothy's father is a Greek (not someone that can help him become a better Christian), Paul invites him along on the journey to learn and grow.

Paul selects someone to mentor who is already expressing an interest in something Paul is proficient at doing. Timothy is a disciple of Jesus. Before we become someone's mentor, we need to make sure we are inviting someone who is sincerely interested in learning from us.

Paul invites Timothy to follow him and learn. In Paul's time, this would have been understood as an invitation to Timothy to be mentored. In our modern culture, it would be awkward to walk up to someone and say, "Hey, I want to mentor you." But we can invite people to help us on a project, come to lunch with us, or spend more time working alongside us. In doing so, a mentoring relationship may develop more organically. Regardless, there needs to be some kind of invitation made for more intentional time together.

2. Do as I Do. Paul teaches Timothy everything he knows. We get evidence of this in Paul's second letter to Timothy: "You have followed my teaching, way of life, purpose, faith, patience, love, endurance, persecutions, and sufferings" (3:10–11). Paul pours everything into Timothy. He wants to make sure that he offers Timothy all of the shortcuts to learning what took Paul years to learn.

When we start to mentor someone, we may be tempted to hold back some of the knowledge we've gained. We may be worried about sharing a particular technique or "life hack" or giving away contact information for clients that has taken us years to curate. While we don't need to disclose every detail of our knowledge right away, eventually we have to hand the keys over. The passing on of inner knowledge is an important part of the mentoring relationship; think about a grandmother finally teaching her grandson the exact ratios in her secret cookie recipe. That can be a sacred moment because the knowledge holds emotional and spiritual weight. More is at play than just a recipe—family history, relationships, and memories come together in the teaching and transitioning. Sometimes our pride causes us to hold some special knowledge back, but that is not what it means to be a mentor. A mentor's goal is to eventually share everything of value with the one being mentored.

3. Lend Your Credibility. When Timothy begins to go out on his own, Paul vouches for him. In his letter to the Philippians, Paul "talks up" Timothy before he is sent to the church in Philippi. When we mentor someone, we likewise need to lend them our credibility. We have a platform and influence that the person we are mentoring does not. Paul shares his influence by making sure that Timothy is accepted when he arrives at Philippi. I've met various people who think they are mentoring someone but refuse to act on behalf of their student in this way. They enjoy having an apprentice but know that if they allow that apprentice to share their platform, it is likely they will lose him. They therefore put a cap on the potential of the person they are teaching.

The best mentors speak well of those they are teaching and use their influence to help their students grow even more. As a mentor, you must lend your credibility to the one you are mentoring.

4. Don't Fear Challenge. Early on in their ministry together, Paul challenges Timothy. In Acts 16 he extends his invitation to Timothy, but in the following chapter he has already left Timothy along with one other person in charge of a church while he is away (17:10–15). Later, Paul places Timothy in charge of the Church in one of the most difficult regions, Ephesus (1 Tm 1:3).

As mentors, we can't fear challenge and we must be ready for failure. Many mentors worry about putting an apprentice in a difficult situation too soon. They are concerned that the stress of the challenge will drive their protégé away. While it is true that a new situation may result in failure, increasing challenge beyond the current capabilities of a person is a necessary part of growth. Timothy was likely stretched in the situations that Paul put him in, but the result was his growth as a man of God and as a minister of the Gospel.

5. Affirm and Encourage. One of the biggest roles of a mentor is to continually affirm and encourage. In the letters Paul sent to Timothy, it is clear that he has no problem offering advice and correction, but he also speaks words of encouragement by reminding Timothy what all of this is for. Paul writes: "Pursue righteousness, devotion, faith, love, patience, and gentleness. Compete well for the faith. Lay hold of eternal life, to which you were called" (1 Tm 6:11–12). Paul reminds Timothy that this ministry is about something bigger than building churches—it is about salvation.

As mentors, we need to affirm and encourage those that follow us, and sometimes that means making sure they remember the big picture. That kind of encouragement can go a long way, especially when work is hard and days are long.

6. Be Equal Partners. There is a line in one of Paul's later letters that reveals a turn in the relationship between Paul and Timothy. It reads, "Timothy, my co-worker, greets you" (Rom 16:21). That phrase, "my co-worker," indicates that Paul now views Timothy as a partner and not a student. This is an important stage in the mentoring relationship: You have elevated someone to be your equal and to be a partner in what you do. They know what you know; they can do what you do. They have risen to the challenge, and you trust them. If you aren't working toward this, then you aren't mentoring someone.

Many leaders are uncomfortable with the idea of a subordinate becoming their equal. I used to struggle thinking about members of my team as eventually being my peers, not because they weren't qualified but because it brought out a lot of insecurities in me. What if they are better than I am at my job? What does that mean for me and my financial security?

When I finally stepped back and recognized that the best legacy I could leave was to equip my team members to be leaders by title or by action, those insecurities melted away. Had I not acknowledged my insecurities, however, those thoughts would have caused me to sabotage my mentorship, and I wouldn't have helped my team grow the way they needed to as leaders.

7. Step Back. The reason we prepare someone to be an equal is that we want them to take our place. That is the next stage of our ultimate goal as mentors—being set aside while another is chosen. At the end of his life, Paul steps back and fully hands the ministry over to Timothy. The second letter to Timothy contains moving and intimate passages from Paul to his co-minister. It is clear that the torch has been passed as Paul approaches what he knows to be his martyrdom, confident that Timothy will continue the ministry.

This is our final goal as mentors—arriving at a place where we are confident stepping back and letting someone else take charge. That mindset requires humility because it means trusting someone with something you've built—and that means allowing them to change it, elevate it, or even destroy it. If we've been chasing humility, we already know that our worth ultimately lies in something greater than what we build. That insight makes it easier to let our work go, trusting that those we've taught will treat it well and make it better than we did.

Weekly Humility Practice

Ask a coworker if there are any small tasks you can help with. You will be surprised that often they ask for help in areas where they see you as skilled and you will have a small opportunity for mentorship.

Monthly Humility Practice

Teach someone a skill that only you know how to do and see how they respond to the experience. If they respond well, be intentional about continuing to teach them. If you are actively mentoring someone, check in with them over coffee and answer any questions they have for you.

Yearly Humility Practice

Think of three people that you could mentor this year, then reach out to them to begin the relationship.

8.
BREAKING
BOUNDARIES

From the desire of being approved,
Deliver me, Jesus.
From the fear of being ridiculed,
Deliver me, Jesus.
That others may become holier than I,
Jesus, grant me the grace to desire it.

I posted a message on Twitter, not thinking much of it. The tweet was rooted in my religious beliefs and spoke to a political situation that was unfolding regarding pro-life causes. I don't have a big platform, but I believe in using it to speak truths about our faith, even when they are hard. I set my phone down and went about the rest of my day.

A few hours later, I checked Twitter and was greeted with an onslaught of notifications. The tweet had gone viral and garnered a lot of responses. A few of them were angry. A few people wanted to argue. Even though it was all digital, it was still anxiety inducing. I am human, and I want to be liked and affirmed; so if people that I don't know are upset with me over social media, I feel the weight of that. Sharing our faith these days is not easy, and it seems to be getting harder with each passing year. What is happening?

Most kids in the United States are now growing up in families that are less religious than a decade or two ago. Many have no religious practice at all. The culture is becoming more secular.

Add to that mix that many people find religion to be a personal matter, and a fear looms: if we invite someone to church with us or speak openly about our faith, we may be mocked, shut down, or even reprimanded. Additionally, people that are faithful and churchgoing may feel they can't answer some of the big questions that come up in conversations about faith, the intersection of religion and politics, or their own walk of discipleship. Fearing getting into a conversation they can't navigate, many people choose to avoid such topics completely. Many keep faith private and personal, but it was never meant to be that way. Our faith is meant to be shared.

This book has been a journey about humility, and much has been practical as it relates to our personal lives, how we view ourselves and others, our work, and our relationships. The final place where we need to embrace humility is in our faith and the ways in which we share it.

FROM THE DESIRE
OF BEING APPROVED

Think about it this way: You discover a new restaurant, and the dishes there change the way you think about food entirely. It becomes your favorite place to go. Everything about it is incredible—the ambience, the menu, the service, and, of course, the actual food. It quickly becomes the spot you take friends when they visit, business clients when they come to town, and your spouse for date night. We share the things that excite us, transform us, or that we just enjoy.

If our faith has been transformative, why don't we share it? We don't have to do so in big, televangelist ways. We can share it by living our lives differently than others or by being ready to answer questions with Christ at the center of our response. Many of us are reluctant to share our faith because we desire the approval of others. That desire can quickly become disordered and lead to pride, which is why we pray against it in the Litany of Humility with the petition *"From the desire of being approved, deliver me, Jesus."*

Too often—whether it is based on a real or imagined result—we believe that sharing our faith will jeopardize our standing in the eyes of others. So we keep our faith—this life-changing reality—to ourselves. Our desire for approval can drive us to withhold the most important parts of ourselves from others, especially if we worry they might be offended. The reality we must accept as Christians is that our faith can sometimes seem offensive.

To be free, we must first admit that we are enslaved. To be saved, we need to humbly admit we need saving. To accept mercy, we have to first acknowledge that we need forgiveness. Many people accept the ideas of being free, being saved, and being shown mercy—but the admissions of being in slavery, needing salvation, and needing forgiveness are more challenging to hear. In fact, to even put forward those ideas can result in ridicule.

FROM THE FEAR
OF BEING RIDICULED

I joined an atheist discussion group online with the intention of "saving" the atheists. I wanted to jump into their discussions and radically proclaim the Gospel to all of them, winning hearts with every keystroke. I quickly realized that one person versus more than 90,000 people on the discussion board was really bad odds. Some people engaged in polite conversation, but many looked for a fight and spent most of their posts mocking me for believing in a "fairytale God." The most common response I received was that "only weak people had faith."

When we tell people about Jesus, we also let people know that we need a savior. This idea contradicts the individualist mindset of our Western culture. We want to believe we don't need anyone to save us, or to be saved from anything we might do. To admit such is to open yourself up to public ridicule. Experiencing ridicule puts us on the outside, and that is a scary place. We are designed for community, so the idea of being ostracized—put outside of the community—elicits a primal fear in us. The Litany of Humility addresses this fear in the petition "*From the fear of being ridiculed, deliver me, Jesus.*"

We may experience ridicule when we stand up for the right thing when it is unpopular. We may experience ridicule simply because another person decides to be cruel at our expense. For our purposes, let's pray about this fear from the standpoint of being ridiculed for our faith. Just as we can keep our faith quiet out of a desire to be approved, we can also avoid sharing it out of a fear of being ridiculed.

Our desire to be approved and our fear of being ridiculed both play into our pride. When we give up or change our convictions in order to gain the approval of others, it means we care more about our image than about our foundations. If we refuse to share our convictions out of a fear of being ridiculed, it means we really aren't that convinced of our beliefs.

To address these two areas where we can grow in humility, we should ask ourselves a simple but challenging question: Do we believe that Jesus Christ makes a difference?

THE QUESTION

The question is easy to respond to automatically. Do you believe that Jesus Christ makes a difference? "Of course," you might be saying; "I'm reading this book, aren't I?" But step back and think about the question. If we really believe that Jesus makes a difference, then aren't we compelled to share him? Many people struggle to share and live their faith because, while it matters to them, it isn't the most important thing. We may look at Jesus as a teacher, dispenser of morality, and good guy. We may even see him as prophetic, but a messiah? That is a different story.

To view Jesus as Messiah, our Savior, we need to be humble. We must admit that we need saving, need mercy, and need to be freed.

TRUE FREEDOM

I once heard a preacher compare the slavery of sin to sitting in a jail cell. Jesus Christ unlocks the cell. He invites us to rise and walk out of the door. But in our pride, we don't believe him. We determine that he must be lying because we've been locked in that cell our whole life. We don't want to look stupid going to what we believe is a locked door. We've accepted our fate and may even feel at home and comfortable in the cell.

St. Paul wrote in a letter to the people in Galatia, "For freedom Christ set us free . . . do not submit again to the yoke of slavery" (Gal 5:1). Jesus sets us free from the slavery of sin. If we've been caught in sin for a long time, though, sin can seem more comfortable than freedom. We may not even want Jesus to set us free. St. Augustine famously prayed, "Lord, make me chaste . . . but not yet." Freedom from sin means saying no to something, namely sin, and sin is inherently selfish. It puts our own wants and desires over those of others. In sin, we prefer ourselves over God. All sin takes its root in pride. When we embrace freedom from sin, we must also embrace humility. We need to admit that we don't hold the key to the cell, but that Christ unlocks it for us. Without him, we are trapped.

Imagine being locked inside that cell but suddenly getting out and experiencing freedom. How would you react? While it might at first be disorienting, you would soon feel joy. Every day out of that cell your joy might grow as you experienced new things—but after a while you would forget about the cell.

Your freedom might start to just feel normal. You may even find yourself going back to another cell, only to need freedom again.

Some people have a life-changing experience or conversion story concerning the moment they were set free for the first time. Reflecting on our conversion story is key to growth in humility because it reminds us that we were set free—and that is a cause for joy. It reminds us that our freedom was actually a mercy from God, one that we didn't earn and don't deserve.

MERCY REIGNS

The reality is you didn't do anything to be set free from that cell. You didn't earn your freedom; to the contrary, you actually deserve to be in the cell. Yet Christ set you free anyway. When there is a disparity of power and one side shows favor, love, or kindness to the other, we call that mercy. An act of mercy involves one individual sharing something with another individual that he or she does not have. In the case of Jesus Christ and all of us, that "thing" is the forgiveness of sins and access to God the Father (and ultimately eternal life in heaven). We don't have that, and nothing we can do will gain that for us. It is a gift. Accepting mercy, though, requires humility. Accepting forgiveness is an act of humility—it requires that we admit that we are wrong.

I once met a young man that told me he never needed forgiveness because he never did anything wrong. His pride was so inflated that he truly believed that he was without fault. What a sad outlook! When we reject mercy because we refuse to admit that we are wrong, we also reject love. An act of mercy is an act of love. As we discussed in chapter 4, St. Paul wrote to the Romans, "God proves his love for us in that while we were still sinners Christ died for us" (5:8). Jesus' death and resurrection were acts of mercy that proved God's love for us. To accept that mercy, we need to humbly admit that we've committed sins that caused Jesus to suffer and die on the Cross.

THAT OTHERS MAY BECOME HOLIER THAN I

Acknowledging those two realities—that we are set free and that we are shown mercy we didn't earn—allows us to really call Jesus our Savior. He is the only one that can set us free, and when we receive that mercy, we experience a love beyond anything we've ever known.

Once we've experienced that, how could we look at someone else trapped in a cell and not share it?

We should reflect on our own freedom and redemption frequently for two reasons. First, it keeps us humble. We can never forget that what we have is a gift from God (see James 1:17). When we start to believe that we have "made ourselves," we enter into pride, and pride shuts us off from who God desires us to be. Second, when we remember Jesus as our Savior, we become more convicted to share him with others, even if it means losing approval or being ridiculed.

This is how we work toward the final petition of the Litany of Humility—*"That others may become holier than I, Jesus, grant me the grace to desire it."* The goal of our existence is simple—to get to heaven and to take as many people there with us as possible. Our lives should convey the love of God in such a way that people come to know something about Christ through us. Our words have the power to direct people toward the one who saved us, but we have to first have the humility to admit that Jesus has saved us and also the humility to face rejection in order to share that message.

TWO FIRES

When Jesus tells his disciples that he must suffer and die, Peter protests. He says that he will never deny Jesus, even if it means his death (see Matthew 26:35). This is the same Peter that walked on water and saw Jesus heal and cast out demons.

He had accompanied Jesus from the beginning. His statement makes sense.

Then Jesus is arrested, and Peter's faith is tested. He follows Jesus at a distance, wanting to be true to his word, but he is also afraid. This fear of suffering the same fate as Jesus comes to the surface as Peter is let into the courtyard and the gatekeeper asks, "You are not one of this man's disciples, are you?" Peter replies, "I am not" (Jn 18:17). Peter is standing near a fire as it happens.

Maybe he has good reason for the denial. He needs to get access to the courtyard, right? He can't help Jesus if he isn't close to him. Maybe this is how Peter justified his words.

Then it happens again. Same question, same response.

Then it happens a third time.

In the Gospel of Mark, it is noted that Peter curses and swears along with his denial (14:71). It is a vehement denial.

Peter is afraid of ridicule and wants to keep the approval of others. We may not be denying our dying Lord, but anytime we avoid sharing our faith and Christian identity in order to maintain the approval of others or avoid ridicule, we deny our faith in a small way.

Thankfully, Jesus promises redemption.

The last chapter of the Gospel of John contains a moving account of Peter reconciling with Jesus. It all begins with a charcoal fire. John includes that detail in describing both Peter's denial of Jesus and his redemption so we connect and compare the two events. As Peter and Jesus walk, Jesus asks Peter three times, "Do you love me?" (Jn 21:15–19). With each response, Peter has an opportunity to make up for his three denials. The final part of the narrative ends with Jesus declaring to Peter, "Follow me."

At least it would seem that way.

The different words the Greeks had for love come into play here, namely, *agape* and *philia*. *Agape*, as we have seen, refers to self-sacrificial love, and *philia* means fraternal love.

A better translation of the Greek would give us this exchange between Jesus and Peter:

Jesus: Simon, son of John, do you love me enough to die for
  me?
Peter: Lord, you know I love you like a brother.
Jesus: Simon, son of John, do you love me enough to die for
  me?
Peter: Lord, you know I love you like a brother.
Jesus: Simon, son of John, do you love me like a brother?
Peter: Yes Lord, you know everything, you know I love you
  like a brother.

John notes before Peter's third response that Peter was sad
because Jesus asked him, "Do you love me like a brother?" Peter
feels he has lost Jesus' approval, because he can't truthfully
respond to Jesus' question of whether Peter loves him enough
to die for him.

In our walk of holiness, it can seem like we are nowhere near
where we want to be. Peter isn't going to make the same mistake
of speaking boldly with words what he can't back up with action.
He loves Jesus, but not the way that Jesus is asking.

That's why Jesus' love is so incredible. Rather than withdraw-
ing his approval when we can't ascend to where we should be,
Jesus comes to meet us. He starts at Peter's level, but doesn't
intend to leave him there. Through the rest of their dialogue,
Jesus assures Peter that while he may not be ready to die for his
faith right now, one day he will be.

The last line, "Follow me," is a call to all of us. Regardless of
where you are in your faith, if you are ready to suffer ridicule for
it or if you struggle to pray that petition, the story arc of Peter's
denial and redemption offers hope. Holiness is a journey, one
that we need to walk well.

LIKE, FOLLOW, SHARE

If we've grown in humility through the preceding chapters, we
can engage in the final practice that will confirm us in that trait—

sharing our faith with others. We need to break the boundaries we've put on our faith so that others can become holier than us. Earlier I wrote that we can't be afraid to become the footnote in someone else's life; our goal should be to become the footnote in the life of a saint.

Think about it—every saint had people who empowered them and mentored them. They had people in their lives who were authentic, confident, grateful, offered praise and rebuke, and showed them the love of God. The saints all had humble people in their lives. Our prayer in the Litany of Humility is that people will become holier than us, and that should mean nothing less than sainthood. There are three things we can do that will help us live this petition and grow in humility as we break boundaries:

1. Remember Your Story with Jesus. In the book of Deuteronomy, Moses gives a series of speeches as the Israelites are about to take possession of the Promised Land. He begins these speeches with the word "remember" (Dt 9:7). God did incredible things for the Israelite people, and Moses wants to make sure they remember that they did not take possession of the Promised Land on their own. It was not the merits or the skill of the people that allowed them to be free; it was the Lord. In the same way, we need to reflect on what God has done for us. This is accomplished through our gratitude journal but also by setting aside time every week to think about our blessings. A great day to do this? Sunday—make it a day to not only worship God but to call to mind the moments when Christ has freed us, shown us mercy, and saved us.

2. Live Your Faith. Don't be afraid to live your faith, and don't change your faith practices based on your audience. If you pray before meals at home, pray before meals at work. If you have guests at your house for dinner, invite them to pray before the meal with you. Schedule your week so you can attend church on Sunday and keep that time of worship a priority. Avoid compromising your spiritual integrity for the sake of making others comfortable or winning approval. In short—practice the humble trait of authenticity.

3. Share the Gospel in Words and Actions. There are several quotes floating around the Internet that are dubiously attributed to saints. One that I find particularly troublesome is attributed to St. Francis: "Let your preaching be your walking." While it is possible St. Francis said that, no credible record exists of it. And although there is nothing wrong with this particular saying, the way in which many people apply it is wrong. We use it as a justification to live our faith but not speak about it. The truth is, if we live our faith well, we will be asked questions about it. When that happens, we need to have a response. St. Peter says this in one of his letters: "Always be ready to give an explanation to anyone who asks you for a reason for your hope" (1 Pt 3:15). We need to walk the walk of faith, but we also need to talk the talk of faith. Eventually we need to be able to tell people about Jesus Christ and what he has done for us.

To keep the faith to ourselves without concern for the salvation and healing of others is potentially one of the highest forms of pride. If you have something good to share, you share it.

If you cultivate the eight aspects of humility we've discussed in this book, you will attract some attention. Your coworkers will wonder why you are more enjoyable to work with and a better leader. Your family will be intrigued by the joyful and authentic disposition with which you approach life. You will feel better. And when questions come about what is different, you can share the hope you've found in Christ.

We must face our fear of ridicule in order to share our faith. That may mean small steps, but Jesus is with us every step of the way. We can walk the path of Peter, sometimes falling and sometimes failing, but always willing to get back up and give what we have. If we are following Jesus and seeking to love him more each day, our ability to break boundaries and share our faith will come more naturally and simply be a part of who we are, how we speak, and the way in which we respond to moments when people need to hear about Jesus. The benefit is worth the risk; a rude response or angry tweet is a brief moment in time, but the salvation of another soul is eternal.

That is a boundary worth breaking.

Weekly Humility Practice

Reflect on the areas where Jesus is calling you to deeper conversion and how those large and small moments are drawing you closer to him.

Monthly Humility Practice

Share your faith with someone close to you or invite them to a church function with you.

Yearly Humility Practice

Remember the date of your big conversion moment or baptism and celebrate it annually.

CONCLUSION

I know of two things that receive a response from the Lord almost immediately when we pray for them: patience and humility. If the Lord responds to prayers for humility immediately, then imagine how quickly he responds when someone starts reading a book about it (or writing one). Humility is foundational to our relationship with Christ. We need to begin with the admission that Jesus is our Savior and we are not. Every prayer must be centered on the phrase "thy will be done," not "my will be done." Contrary to what many in the world tell us, humility brings freedom.

To live these eight attributes of humility and really work on them is to run countercultural to what many people will tell you brings success. I hope these chapters have inspired you and that the weekly, monthly, and yearly practices will challenge you to strive for the kind of humble life that sets us free. Humility is the unlikely foundation of success—we just need to bear in mind that it might not be success as the world defines it.

When we live authentically, we find success in our relationships because we can be who we really are. We become better leaders because we allow ourselves to be vulnerable rather than narcissistic. We grow deeper in our relationship with the Lord because we allow God to tell us who we are and we find freedom in that truth.

When we grow in confidence, we worry less about impressing other people. Our relationships improve because we care more about others than about being liked. We become more effective and successful leaders because we don't base our worth solely in what people think about us, but in who God calls us to be.

Our relationship with Christ grows because we walk boldly by his grace, rather than relying on our own merits.

When we are grateful, we stop comparing ourselves to others and are free of envy. We become better leaders because we aren't chasing the next honor or accolade but are content with simply doing good work. If we recognize the many blessings that God brings us, we are continually in awe of his love.

When we make loving others our goal, we are free to give ourselves to others without worrying about what we are going to get. Our leadership style is marked by compassion rather than fear, and we can take the love that God has so generously poured out on us and pour it out on others.

When we give praise, we are more open to accepting criticism in our relationships and as leaders. We can honestly stand before God as sinners in need of mercy.

When we empower those around us, we get to be a footnote in their story, and success becomes less about recognition and more about helping someone be who God wants them to be. Our relationships are grounded in humility, we share leadership with others, and we embrace the reality that God has chosen us as vessels to work miracles.

When we become mentors, we slowly reduce our pride and we pass on our knowledge so that we may one day be joyfully set aside, confident that we have helped someone grow to be better than we were.

When we break boundaries, we share our faith in order to help others become holy and discover freedom in Christ. We may even help change their eternity.

These eight practices help us become humble in the right ways. They help us imagine anew what success looks like while giving us freedom. We don't have to climb the ladder anymore; we get to enjoy the journey of life.

Consider what really brings joy—is it money? Fame? Affirmation? Being the preference of others? Those things may give us temporary happiness, but what brings us lasting joy is a meaningful relationship with God, our Creator, and the ability to have healthy relationships with other people. Joy in work comes from doing a job well and honestly, while raising other people up to do *your* job even better. Ask a teacher at their retirement what the best part of their work was, and dedicated teachers will tell you it was watching their students go on to do great things. Those moments bring lasting joy. Our fame is fleeting, but if we can change a life, we get to hold on to that forever.

LIFELONG JOURNEY

Chasing humility is a constant process, and there is always space for improvement. We are human, and our resolve will be tested. Through different seasons of life, you may find that you struggle more with authenticity and confidence than with giving praise or mentoring. Our spiritual life is not stagnant. We work through ebbs and flows as the Lord continues to mold our hearts. Committing to the great spiritual work of humility is a necessary endeavor for anyone who wants to experience a joy and freedom that worldly success cannot provide. Striving for this kind of humility puts our accomplishments into perspective and detaches us from material wealth. In a world that is increasingly individualistic and self-absorbed, the humble women and men stand out (even though they probably don't want to).

You can become one of those people that stand out. But be careful what you ask for. Within the few short months that I composed this book, the Lord presented me with ample opportunities to grow in humility. I should have expected as much, and I found myself more aware of my responses to situations where I was passed over or gossiped about, or when I simply dropped the ball and had to apologize. I will say from experience that living humility has at times been about as fun as a six-hour visit to the dentist, but it has also made me a more joyful, level-headed person.

We need humble people living their faith. So become one. Take the process day by day, be mindful of where you trip up, and commit to doing better tomorrow. Perhaps we can take final inspiration for the legacy we want to leave from the author of the Litany of Humility.

Many attribute the Litany of Humility to Rafael Cardinal Merry del Val, the secretary of state for Pope Pius X. The process of canonization for Merry del Val has begun, and he is now called a "Servant of God." Evidence for his authorship of the prayer comes from a letter written in 1948 by C. S. Lewis. If you look at a copy of the prayer, it may even bear Merry del Val's name. But he isn't the original author.

The cardinal likely added to an existing prayer, the "Litany to Obtain Holy Humility." You can easily find this version of the prayer online in a free ebook that is now public domain. This book was published in 1867 under the title *The Fervent Adorer*, by an author using the pen name "ARC Clergyman." It bears many of the same petitions of the modern Litany of Humility as well as some additional petitions and intercessory prayers that Merry del Val omitted in his version.

Since the original was written under a pen name, the identity of the author is unknown. Among the many prayers in *The Fervent Adorer*, the Litany to Obtain Holy Humility lives on as one of the most widely read prayers in its adapted form. It is oddly consoling that, whoever the author is, his petitions were heard and received. His name was ultimately forgotten, and he will never be known as the author of this prayer, his work ultimately modified and attributed to someone else.

Could you accept that if it meant sanctity? Would you be willing to be the footnote in the life of someone else if it meant that they became a recognized saint? Could you find joy in simply being authentically who God called you to be, knowing that a relationship with Christ was the greatest reward you could ever receive? I am confident that "ARC Clergyman" received his reward for the fruits that many would receive from his simple prayer. I am confident that the task of humility is a worthy one that we can undertake under his example as well. I am confident that the fruit of that task is real joy, authentic love, and great hope in a God that hears our prayers for humility and loves us enough to answer them right away.

Humility is not an option for the Christian; the speaker I heard all those years ago got that right. It is the very foundation of our relationship with Christ and with others, and is critical in the ways we will be called to lead. We can go through life without chasing humility, but we will find ourselves exhausted by standing still. To chase humility is to find life. We become lighter as we engage in the chase because we shed so much of what has held us down. Humility becomes easier as we practice it, and if we practice it well, we become less aware we are practicing it at all. It simply becomes who we are.

If you are ready to be transformed in a way that doesn't leave you lacking but makes you more, then it is time to embrace humility.

If you want to find real success in your relationships, work, and spiritual life, then it is time to live humility.

If you are tired of being weighed down, running the same race only to go to bed at night wondering if there is something more, then it is time to start chasing humility.

A new life is waiting for you, and it begins with humility.

Let the chase begin.

JOEL STEPANEK is director of resource development at Life Teen. He is the author or coauthor of several Life Teen books, including *Getting More Out of Confession, True North,* and *Greatest Job on Earth.* He is a ministry team member and keynote speaker for the Steubenville Youth Conferences.

Stepanek earned a bachelor's degree in religious studies from the University of Wisconsin in 2007. In 2015, he earned a master's degree in religion and religious education with an emphasis in youth and young adult ministry from Fordham University. He previously served as director of youth ministry at St. Francis of Assisi Parish in Manitowoc, Wisconsin, and is an adjunct faculty member at Franciscan University of Steubenville.

Stepanek and his wife, Colleen, live in Gilbert, Arizona, with their children.

Facebook: joelstepanek
Instagram: @LT_JStepanek
Twitter: @LT_JStepanek

AVE

AVE MARIA PRESS

Founded in 1865, Ave Maria Press,
a ministry of the Congregation of
Holy Cross, is a Catholic publishing
company that serves the spiritual and
formative needs of the Church and its
schools, institutions, and ministers;
Christian individuals and families; and
others seeking spiritual nourishment.

For a complete listing of titles from

Ave Maria Press

Sorin Books

Forest of Peace

Christian Classics

visit www.avemariapress.com

AVE MARIA PRESS
Notre Dame, IN

A Ministry of the United States Province of Holy Cross